All Beset by Birth, Decay, and Death

Twelve Dhamma Talks on Practice
given to the Nuns and Anāgārikās
at Parappuduwa Nuns Island

by
Sister Ayyā Khemā

BUDDHIST PUBLICATION SOCIETY
KANDY • SRI LANKA

Buddhist Publication Society
P.O. Box 61
54 Sangharaja Mawatha
Kandy
Sri Lanka
http://www.bps.lk

Copyright © 1988 Sister Ayyā Khemā
First BPS edition: 2008

Published with the kind permission of
Jhana Verlag, Germany.

National Library of Sri Lanka—Cataloguing in Publication Data

Ayya Khema
  All of Us: Beset by Birth, Decay and Death/ Ayya Khema. - Kandy: Buddhist Publication Society Inc., 2008.- p.94; 21cm.

ISBN 978-955-24-0325-5	Price Rs.
i. 294.34435 DDC 21	ii. Title
1. Meditation - Buddhism	

Printed in Sri Lanka by
Ruchira Printers
Kandy—Sri Lanka

Contents

Appreciation iv

Preface v

I. The Dhamma of the Blessed One is Perfectly Expounded 1

II. Accepting Ourselves 8

III. To Control Our Mind 16

IV. Be Nobody 22

V. War and Peace 28

VI. Truth 35

VII. Renunciation 40

VIII. Ideal Solitude 44

IX. Dukkha for Knowledge and Vision 51

X. Our Underlying Tendencies 58

XI. Sorrowless, Stainless and Secure 67

XII. Path and Fruit 71

Glossary 81

APPRECIATION

My thanks go to all the nuns, anāgārikās, laymen and women who have listened time and again to my expositions of the Buddha's teachings.

Without them, these talks would not have happened and this little booklet would not be possible.

A very special "thank you" to my friends, who have encouraged and supported my work and the publication of this book by their continued understanding and generosity.

Those who have typed the manuscript from tapes made during the talks have given freely of their time, energy and love to the propagation of the Dhamma.

May everyone connected with this joint undertaking reap the excellent kamma resulting from the gift of assistance.

Sister Ayyā Khemā
Parappuduwa Nuns Island
Dodanduwa, Sri Lanka
1 January 1987

PREFACE

This little volume is offered to all people everywhere who know *dukkha*, which is not only suffering, pain and grief, but all the unsatisfactoriness all of us experience during our lifetime.

It is that unfulfilled striving in heart and mind which keeps pushing us in so many directions to find the ultimate satisfaction.

When we have realized that all the avenues we have tried have brought us to a dead end, then the time has come to turn to Buddha's teachings and see for ourselves whether his promise, "there's only one thing I teach: suffering and its end" can be experienced within ourselves and whether fulfilment is possible.

As practice progresses, we will find that by letting go of our preconceived ideas on how and where *dukkha* can be avoided, we come upon uncharted landscapes within ourselves, which provide a totally new concept of life, its purpose, its value and its ultimate reality.

May there be many "with little dust in their eyes" who can turn the tide on *dukkha* and be liberated.

Sister Ayyā Khemā

I. THE DHAMMA OF THE BLESSED ONE IS PERFECTLY EXPOUNDED

> The Dhamma of the Blessed One
> Is perfectly expounded,
> To be seen here and now,
> Not a matter of time.

The first line of this chant proclaims real faith in the Dhamma: not believing everything without inquiring, but developing an inner relationship of trust. When we are faithful to someone, then we also trust that person, we give ourselves into his or her hands, have a deep connection and an inner opening. How much more is this true of the faith in the teaching of the Buddha. Those aspects of the Dhamma which we don't as yet understand can be left in abeyance. Nevertheless this does not shake our faith and trust.

If we feel that it is "perfectly expounded", then we are very fortunate, for we know one thing in this universe that is perfect. There's nothing else to be found that's without blemish, nor is there anything that is becoming perfect. If we have that trust, faithfulness and love towards the Dhamma and believe it to be perfectly expounded, then we have found something beyond compare. We are blessed with an inner wealth.

"To be seen here and now" is up to each of us. The Dhamma has been made clear by the Enlightened One who taught it out of compassion, but we have to see it ourselves with an inner vision.

All of Us

"Here and now" needs to be stressed, because it means not forgetting but being aware of the Dhamma in each moment. This awareness helps us to watch our reactions before they result in unskilful words or actions, seeing the positive within us and cultivating it, and seeing the negative and substituting it. When we believe all our thoughts and claim justification for them, we're not seeing the Dhamma. There are no justifications, there are only arising phenomena which cease again.

"Not a matter of time" means that we are not dependent upon a Buddha being alive in order to practise the Dhamma; though this is a widespread belief, it is quite possible to practise right now. Some people think there has to be a perfect situation or a perfect teacher or perfect meditation. None of that is true. Mental and physical phenomena (*dhammas*) are constantly coming and going, changing without pause. When we hang onto them and consider them ours, then we will believe any story our minds tell us, without discrimination. We consist of body, feelings, perceptions, mental formations and consciousness, which we grip tightly and believe them to be "me" and "mine." We need to take a step back and be a neutral observer of the whole process.

"Inviting one to come and see, leading inwards." means that the understanding of the Dhamma leads us into our inner depth. We are not invited to come and see a meditation hall or a Buddha statue, a stupa or a shrine. Rather, we are invited to come and see the phenomena (*dhammas*) arising within us. The defilements as well as the purifications are to be found inside our own heart and mind.

The Dhamma of the Blessed

Our minds are very busy, always remembering, planning, hoping or judging. This body could also be very busy picking up little stones and throwing them into the water all day long, but we would consider that a foolish expenditure of energy, and we direct the body towards something useful. We need to do the same with the mind. Instead of thinking about this and that, allowing the defilements to arise, we could also direct the mind towards something beneficial, such as investigating our likes and dislikes, our desires and rejections, our ideas and views.

When the mind inquires, it doesn't get involved in its own creations. It can't do both at the same time. As it becomes more and more observant, it remains objective for longer periods of time. That's why the Buddha taught that mindfulness is the one way for the purification of beings. The clear and lucid observation of all arising phenomena eventually shows that there are only phenomena manifesting as mind and body, which are constantly expanding and contracting in the same way as the universe does. Unless we become very diligent observers, we will not see that aspect of mind and body and will not know the Dhamma "here and now," even though we have been "invited to come and see."

"To be known by the wise, each for themselves" means that no one can know the Dhamma for another. We can chant, read, discuss and listen, but unless we watch all that arises, we will not know the Dhamma by ourselves. There's only one place where Dhamma can be known and that's in our own heart and mind. It has to be a personal experience that comes about through constant observation of ourselves. Meditation helps. Unless we inquire into our own reactions and know why we want one thing and reject another, we haven't seen Dhamma. Then the mind will also get a clear perception of impermanence (*anicca*) because our desires and dislikes are constantly changing. We'll see that the mind which is thinking and the body which is breathing are both painful (*dukkha*).

When the mind doesn't operate with an uplifted, transcending awareness, it creates suffering (*dukkha*). Only a measureless, illumined mind is free from that. The body certainly produces *dukkha* in many ways through its inability to remain steady. Seeing this clearly will give us a strong determination to know Dhamma by ourselves.

Wisdom arises from within and comes from an inner knowing, an understood experience, which creates self-confidence. Neither knowledge nor listening can bring it about. Wisdom also means maturity, which has nothing to do with age. Sometimes ageing may help, but it doesn't always. We need not look for somebody else's confirmation and goodwill—we know with certainty.

When we chant anything at all, it is vital that we know the meaning of the words and inquire whether they have any relevance to us.

> *Pamādamūlako lobho, lobho vivādamūlako,*
> *dāsabyakārako lobho, lobho paramhi petiko,*
> *taṃ lobhaṃ parijānantaṃ vande'haṃ*
> *vītalobhakaṃ.*
>
> Greed is the root of negligence, greed's the root of strife,
> Greed enslavement brings about, and in the future ghostly birth;

That One who's known greed to the end,
I honour Him who's free of greed.

Vihaññamūlako doso, doso virūpakārako.
vināsakārako doso, doso paramhi nerayo,
taṃ dosaṃ parijānantaṃ vande'haṃ
vītadosakaṃ.

Hate's the root of turbulence, of ugliness the cause,
Hate causes much destruction and in the future hellish birth;
That One who's known hate to the end, I honour Him who's free of hate.

sabbaghamūlako moho, moho sabbītikārako,
sabbandhakārako moho, moho paramhi svādiko
taṃ mohaṃ parijānantaṃ vande'haṃ
vītamohakaṃ.

Delusion's the root of every ill, delusion's a troublemaker,
All blinding from delusion comes, and in the future birth as beast;
That One who's known delusion's end, I honour Him, delusion-free.

The Buddha said:

> Better than a thousand sayings,
> Consisting of meaningless lines,
> is the single meaningful line,
> which hearing one becomes calm.

Dhp 100

All of Us

If we can practise one line of Dhamma, it's so much more valuable than knowing the whole chanting book by heart.

The constant arising and ceasing of phenomena, which are our teachers, never take a rest. Dhamma is being taught to us constantly. All our waking moments are Dhamma teachers, if we can see them to be so. The Dhamma is the truth expounded by the Enlightened One, which is the law of nature surrounding us and imbedded within us.

Once the Buddha said: "Ānanda, it is owing to my being a good friend to them that living beings subject to birth are freed from birth" (SN 45:2).

Everyone needs a good friend who has enough selflessness not only to be helpful, but also to point out when we are slipping. Treading the Dhamma path is like walking a tightrope. It leads along us straight line and every time we slip, we hurt. If we have a painful feeling inside, we're no longer on the tightrope of the Dhamma. Our good friend (*kalyāṇamitta*) might say to us, then: "You stepped too far to the right, or to the left (whatever the case may be). You weren't careful, that's why you fell into depression and pain. I'll point out to you when you're slipping next time." We can only accept this from someone whom we trust and have confidence in.

We can be fooled by a person's beautiful words or splendid appearance. The character of a person is shown not only in words, but in the small day-to-day activities. One of the very important guidelines to a person's character is how they react when things go wrong. It's easy to be loving, helpful and friendly when everything goes well, but when difficulties arise, our endurance and patience are tested as well as our equanimity and

The Dhamma of the Blessed

determination. The less ego-consciousness we have, the easier we can handle all situations.

At first, when we start to walk on the tightrope of the Dhamma path, it may feel uncomfortable. We aren't used to balancing ourselves, but rather to swaying all over the place, going in all directions, wherever it's most comfortable. We may feel restricted and coerced, not being allowed to live according to our natural instincts. Yet in order to walk on a tightrope, we have to restrict ourselves in many ways with mindfulness. These restrictions may at first feel irksome, like fetters or bonds; later they turn out to be the liberating factors.

To have this perfect jewel of the Dhamma in our hearts, we need to be awake and aware. Then we can prove by our own watchfulness that "the Dhamma of the Blessed One is perfectly expounded." There is no worldly jewel that can match the value of the Dhamma. Each one of us can become the owner of this priceless gem. We can call ourselves most fortunate to have such an opportunity. When we wake up in the morning, let that be our first thought: "What good fortune it is for me to practise the Dhamma."

II. Accepting Ourselves

It's a strange phenomenon how difficult people find it to love themselves. One would think it is the easiest thing in the world, because we're constantly concerned with ourselves. We're always interested in how much we can get, how well we can perform, how comfortable we can be. The Buddha mentioned in a discourse that "oneself is dearest to oneself." So with all that, why is it so difficult to actually love ourselves?

Loving ourselves certainly doesn't mean indulging ourselves. Really loving is an attitude towards ourselves that most people don't have, because they know quite a few things about themselves that are not desirable. Everyone has innumerable attitudes, reactions, likes and dislikes that they'd be better off without. Judgment is made and while we like our positive attitudes, we dislike the others. With that comes suppression of those aspects of ourselves that we are not pleased with. We don't want to know about them and don't acknowledge them. That's one way of dealing with ourselves that is detrimental to growth.

Another unskilful way is to dislike the part of ourselves that appears negative. Every time it arises we blame ourselves, which makes matters twice as bad as they were before. With that comes fear and very often aggression. If we want to deal with ourselves in a balanced way, it's not useful to pretend that the unpleasant part doesn't exist, those aggressive, irritable, sensual, conceited tendencies. If we pretend, then we are far from reality, and put a split into ourselves. Even though one may be totally sane, the appearance given is that of not being quite real. We've all come across people like that, who are too sweet to be true, as a result of pretence and suppression.

Blaming ourselves doesn't work either. In both instances we transfer our own reactions to other people. We blame others for their deficiencies, real or imagined, or we don't see them as ordinary human beings. Everyone lives in an unreal world, meaning it's ego-deluded, but this world of likes and dislikes is particularly unreal, because everything is considered either as perfectly wonderful or absolutely terrible.

The only thing that is real is that we have six roots within us: three roots of good and three roots of evil. The latter are greed, hate and delusion, but we also have their opposites: generosity, loving-kindness and wisdom. They are the underlying roots of everyone's behaviour. Take an interest in this matter. If we investigate this and don't get anxious about it, then we can easily accept these six roots in everybody—with no difficulty at all. When we have seen them in ourselves, then we can look at ourselves a little more realistically, not blaming ourselves for the unwholesome roots, not patting ourselves on the back for the wholesome ones, but rather accepting their existence within us. We can also accept others more clear-sightedly and have a much easier time relating to them.

Then, we will also not suffer from disappointments and we won't blame, because we won't live in a world where only black and white exist in either the three roots of unwholesomeness or their opposites. Such a world doesn't exist anywhere, and the only person to be like that is an Arahant. It's largely a matter of degree in everyone else. These degrees of good and evil are so finely tuned, there's so little difference within the degrees in each one of us, that it really doesn't matter. All of us have the same job to do: to cultivate the wholesome tendencies and uproot the unwholesome ones.

Outwardly it seems as though we're all different, but on closer inspection this is an illusion. We're all having the same problems and we also have the same faculties to deal with them. The only difference is the length of training that we have had. Training which may have been going on for a number of lifetimes has brought about a little more clarity. That's all!

Clarity of thinking comes from purification of our emotions, which is a difficult job that needs to be done. It can only be done successfully when it is not an emotional upheaval, but a clear-cut, straightforward job that we do on ourselves. When it is seen to be just that, it takes the sting out of it. The charge of "I'm so wonderful" or "I'm so terrible" is defused, for we are neither wonderful nor terrible. Everyone is a human being with all the potential and all the obstructions. If we can love that human being, the one that is "me" with all its faculties and tendencies, then we can love others realistically, usefully and helpfully. But if we split the parts and love only the part that is nice and dislike the part which isn't nice enough, we are never going to come to grips with reality. One day we'll have to see it for what it is. It's a "working ground," a *kammaṭṭhāna*, a straightforward and interesting affair of our own heart.

Accepting Ourselves

If we look at ourselves in this manner, we will learn to love ourselves in a wholesome way. "Just as a mother at the risk of life, loves and protects her child...," become your own mother! If we want to have a relationship with ourselves that is realistic and conducive to growth, then we need to become our own mother. A sensible mother can distinguish between that which is useful for her child and that which is detrimental, but she doesn't stop loving the child when it misbehaves. This may be the most important aspect to look at in ourselves. Everyone, at one time or another, misbehaves in thought, speech, and action; most frequently in thought, fairly frequently in speech, and less often in action. So what do we do with that? What does a mother do? She tells the child not to do it again; she loves the child as much as she's always loved it, and just gets on with the job of bringing up the child. Maybe we can, too, start to bring up ourselves.

The whole of this training is a matter of maturing. Maturity is wisdom, which is unfortunately not connected to age. If it were, it would be very easy, then we would have a guarantee, but since it isn't, it's hard work, a job to be done. First comes recognition, then learning not to condemn, but to understand that "This is the way it is." The third step is change. Recognition may be the hardest part for most people; it's not easy to see what goes on inside of ourselves. This is the most important and the most interesting aspect of contemplation.

We lead a contemplative life, but that does not mean we sit in meditation all day long. A contemplative life means that we consider every aspect of what happens as part of a learning experience. We remain introspective

All of Us

under all circumstances. When we become outgoing, with what the Buddha termed "exuberance of youth," we go to the world with our thoughts, speech and action. We need to recollect ourselves and return within. A contemplative life in some orders is a life of prayer, but in our way it's a combination of meditation and lifestyle. The contemplative life goes on inside of ourselves. We can do the same thing with or without recollection. Contemplation is the most important aspect of introspection. It isn't necessary to sit still all day and watch our breath. Every move, every thought, every word can give rise to understanding ourselves.

This kind of work on ourselves will bring about deep inner security that is rooted in reality. Most people are wishing and hoping for this kind of security, but are not even able to voice their longing. Living in a myth, constantly hoping or being afraid, is opposed to having inner strength. The feeling of security arises when we see reality inside of ourselves, and thereby the reality in everyone else, and come to terms with it.

Let us accept the fact that the Buddha knew the truth when he said everybody has seven underlying tendencies: sensual desire, ill-will, speculative views, sceptical doubt, conceit, craving for continued existence, and ignorance. Find them in yourself. Smile at them; do not burst into tears because of them. Smile and say: "Well, there you are. I'll do something about you."

The contemplative life is often lived heavy-handedly. A certain lack of joy is compensated for by being outgoing. This doesn't work. We should cultivate a light-heartedness and still stay within ourselves. There's nothing to be worried or fearful about, nothing that is too difficult. Dhamma means the law of nature, and we are manifesting this law of nature all the time. What can there be to get away from? We cannot escape the law of nature. Wherever we are, we are the Dhamma, we are impermanent (*anicca*), unfulfilled (*dukkha*), and of no core substance (*anattā*). It doesn't matter whether we sit here or on the moon. It's always the same. So we need a light-hearted approach to our own difficulties and those of everyone else, but not exuberance and outpouring. Rather a constant inwardness containing a bit of amusement. This works best. If we have a sense of humour about ourselves, it is much easier to love ourselves properly. It's also much easier to love everybody else.

There used to be a television show in America, called "People are Funny." We do have the oddest reactions. When they are analyzed and taken apart, they are often found to be absurd. We have very strange desires and wishes and unrealistic images of ourselves. It's quite true, people are funny, so why not see that side of ourselves? It makes it easier to accept that which we find so unacceptable in ourselves and others.

There is one aspect of human life which we cannot change, namely, that it keeps on happening moment after moment. We've all been meditating here for some time. What does the world care? It just keeps on going. The only one who cares, who gets perturbed, is our own heart and mind. When there is perturbance, upheaval, unreality and absurdity, then there is also unhappiness. This is quite unnecessary. Everything just is. If we learn to approach all happenings with more equanimity by being accepting, then the work of purification is much easier.

All of Us

This is our work, our own purification, and it can only be done by each one for him- or herself.

One of the best aspects about it is that if we remember what we are doing, keep at it day after day without forgetting and continuing to meditate, not expecting great results, little by little it does happen. That, too, just is. As we keep working at it, there is a constant chipping away at the defilements and at the unreal thinking, because there is no happiness in that and few want to hang on to unhappiness. Eventually we run out of things to do outside of ourselves: the books are all saying the same things; the letters have all been written; the flowers have all been watered. There's nothing left except to look inside. As this happens again and again, a change takes place. It may be slow, but when we have been here so many lifetimes, what's a day, a month, a year, ten years? They're all just happening.

There's nothing else to do and there's nowhere else to go. The earth is moving in a circle, life is moving from birth to death without us having to move at all. It's all happening without our help. The only thing we need to do is to see reality for what it truly is. Then when we do, we will find that loving ourselves and loving others is a natural outcome of that. Because we are concerned with reality, and that is the heart's real work—to love—but only if we've also seen the other side of the coin in ourselves and have done the work of purification. Then it is no longer an effort or a deliberate attempt, but it becomes a natural function of our inner feelings: inwardly directed but shining outwards.

The inward direction is an important aspect of our contemplative life. Whatever happens inwardly has direct

Accepting Ourselves

repercussions on what takes place outwardly. The inner light and purity cannot be hidden; nor can the defilements.

We sometimes think we can portray something we are not. That is not possible. The Buddha said that we only know a person after having heard him speak many times and having lived with him for a long time. People generally try to show themselves off as something better than they really are. Then, of course, they become disappointed in themselves when they fail, and equally disappointed in others. To realistically know ourselves makes it possible to truly love. That kind of feeling gives a certain light-heartedness needed for this job in which we're engaged. By accepting ourselves and others as we truly are, the job of purification, chipping away at the defilements, is made much easier.

III. To Control Our Mind

Our old friend, *dukkha*, arises in the mind as dissatisfaction caused by all sorts of triggers. It can be triggered by bodily discomfort, but more often it is caused by the mind's own aberrations and convolutions. The mind creates *dukkha*, and that is why we must really watch and guard our minds.

Our own mind can make us happy—or unhappy. There is no person or thing in the whole world that will do this for us. All happenings act as triggers for us, which constantly catch us unawares. Therefore we need to develop strong awareness of our own mind states.

We have a good chance of doing that in meditation. There are two directions in meditation: calm (*samatha*) and insight (*vipassanā*). If we can achieve some calm, this indicates that concentration is improving, but unless that valuable skill is used for insight, it is a waste of time. If the mind becomes calm, joy often arises, yet we must observe how fleeting and impermanent that joy is, and how even bliss is essentially still only a condition which can be easily lost. Only insight is irreversible. The stronger the calm established, the better it will withstand disturbances. In the beginning any noise, discomfort or thought will disturb the calm, especially if the mind has not been calm during the day.

Impermanence (*anicca*) needs to be seen quite clearly in everything that happens, whether it is in or out of meditation. The fact of constant change should and must be used for gaining insight into reality. Mindfulness is the heart of Buddhist meditation and insight is its goal. We're spending our time in many different ways and some portion of it in meditation, but all our time can be used to gain some insight into our own mind. That's where our whole world is happening, unfolding. Nothing, except what we are thinking, exists for us.

The more we watch our minds and see what it does to us and for us, the more we will be inclined to take good care of it and treat it with respect. One of the biggest mistakes we can make is taking the mind for granted. The mind has the capacity to create both good and evil for us, and only when we are able to remain happy and even-minded, no matter what conditions are arising, only then can we say that we have gained a little control. Until then we are out of control and our thoughts are our master.

> Whatever harm a foe may do to foe,
> Or hater unto one he hates,
> The ill-directed mind indeed
> Can do one greater harm.
>
> What neither mother, nor father too,
> Nor any other relative can do,
> The well-directed mind indeed
> Can do one greater good.
>
> Dhp 42, 43 [Khantipālo, trans.]

These words of the Buddha show quite clearly that there is nothing more valuable than a controlled and skilfully-directed mind. Taming our mind does not happen only in meditation; that is just one specific training. It can be likened to learning to play tennis. We

All of Us

work out with a trainer, again and again, until we have found our balance and aptitude, and can actually play in a tennis match. Our training for taming the mind happens in day-to-day living, in all the situations we encounter.

The greatest support we can have is mindfulness, which means being totally present in each moment. If the mind remains centred, then it can't make up stories about the injustice of the world or our friends, or about our desires, or our lamentations. All these mind-made stories would fill many volumes, but we are mindful such verbalizations stop. "Mindful" is being fully absorbed in the moment, leaving no room for anything else. We are filled with the momentary happening, whether that may be standing or sitting or lying down, being comfortable or uncomfortable, experiencing pleasant or unpleasant feelings. Whatever it may be, it is a non-judgmental awareness, "knowing only," without evaluation.

Clear comprehension brings evaluation. We comprehend the purpose of our thought, speech or action, whether we are using skilful means or not, and whether we have actually achieved the required results. We need some distance from ourselves in order to be able to evaluate dispassionately. If we are right in the middle, it's very difficult to get an objective view. Mindfulness coupled with clear comprehension provides us with the necessary distance, objectivity, and dispassion.

Any *dukkha* that we experience, whether small, medium or large, continuous or intermittent, is all created by our mind. We are the creators of all that happens to us, forming our own destiny; nobody else is involved. Everyone one else is playing their own role; we just happen to be near some people and farther away from others. But whatever we are doing, everything is due to our own mind states.

The more we watch our thoughts in meditation, if there is an objective viewing of what is happening the more insight can arise.. When we watch mind states arising, staying and ceasing, we detach from our thinking process, and this brings dispassion. Thoughts are coming and going all the time, just like the breath. If we hang on to them, try to keep them, that's when all the trouble starts. We want to own them and really do something with them, especially if they are negative ones, which is then bound to create *dukkha*.

The Buddha's formula for the highest effort is worth remembering:

Not to let an unwholesome thought arise that has not yet arisen;

Not to sustain an unwholesome thought that has already arisen;

To arouse a wholesome thought that has not yet arisen; and

To sustain a wholesome thought that has already arisen.

The quicker we can become a master of this effort the better. This is part of the training we undergo in meditation. When we have learned to quickly drop whatever is arising in meditation, then we can do the same with unwholesome thoughts in daily living. When we are alert to an unwholesome thought in meditation, we can use the same skill to protect our minds at all times. The more we learn to shut our mind-door to all negativities which disturb our inner peace, the easier our life becomes. Peace of mind is not indifference. A peaceful mind is a compassionate mind. Recognizing and letting go is not suppression. *Dukkha* is self-made and self-perpetuated. If we are sincere in wanting to get rid of it, we have to watch the mind carefully, to get an insight into what's really happening within. What is triggering us? There are innumerable triggers, but there are only two reactions: one is equanimity, the other is craving.

We can learn from everything. Today some anāgārikas had to wait quite a long time in the bank, which was an exercise in patience. Whether the exercise was successful or not doesn't matter as much as that it was a learning experience. Everything we do is an exercise; this is our purpose as human beings. It's the only reason for being here, namely to use the time on our little planet for learning and growing. It can be called an adult education class. Everything else we can think of as the purpose of life is a mistaken view.

We're guests here, giving a limited guest performance. If we use our time to gain insight into ourselves utilizing our likes and dislikes, our resistances, our rejections, our worries, our fears, then we're spending this lifetime to the best advantage. It's a great skill to live in such a way. The Buddha called it "urgency" (*saṃvega*), a sense of having to work on ourselves now, and not leave it for some future unspecified date when we might have more time. Everything can be a learning experience, and the only time is now.

When we meet our old friend *dukkha*, we should ask: "Where did you come from?" When we get an answer, we should inquire again, getting deeper into the subject. There's only one true answer, but we won't get it immediately. We have to go through several answers until we get to the bottom line, which is "ego." When we've come to that one, we know we have come to the end of the questioning and to the beginning of insight. We can then try to see how the ego has produced *dukkha* again. What did it do, how did it react? When we see the cause, it may be possible to let go of that particular wrong view. Having seen cause and effect by ourselves, we'll never forget it again.

Single drops fill a bucket; little by little we purify. Every moment is worthwhile. The more we experience every moment as worthwhile, the more energy there is. There are no useless moments, every single one is important if we use it skilfully. Enormous energy arises from that, because all of it adds up to a life which is lived in the best possible way.

IV. Be Nobody

Being happy also means being peaceful, but quite often people don't really want to direct their attention to that. There is the connotation of "not interesting" about it, or "not enough happening." Obviously, there would be no proliferations (*papañca*) or excitement.

Peace is thought of as an absolute in this world, from a political, social and personal angle. Yet peace is very hard to find anywhere. One of the reasons must be that not only is it difficult to attain, but also very few people work for such an achievement. It seems as if it were a negation of life, of our own supremacy. Only those who practise a spiritual discipline would care to direct their minds towards peace.

It is a natural tendency to cultivate our own superiority, but it also often falls into the other extreme, our own inferiority. When we have our own superiority in mind, it's impossible to find peace. The only thing that we can find is a power game: "Anything you can do, I can do better." Or, at times, when it's quite obvious that this isn't so, then "anything you can do, I can't do as well." There are moments of truth in everyone's life, when we see quite clearly that we can't do everything as well as the next person, whether it's sweeping a path or writing a book.

This kind of stance, which is very common, is the opposite of peacefulness. A display of either our own abilities, or the lack of them, will produce restlessness rather than peace. There's always the reaching out, the craving for a result in the form of other people's admittance of our own superiority or their denial of it. When they deny it, there is warfare; when they admit to it, there is victory.

Victory over other people has as its underlying cause a battle. In war there is never a winner; there are only losers. No matter who signs the peace treaty first, both sides lose. The same applies to this kind of attitude. There are only losers, even though we may have a momentary victory, having been accepted as the one who knows better, or is stronger or cleverer. War and peace do not go well together.

One wonders in the end: does anybody really want peace? Nobody seems to have it. Is anybody really trying to get it? We do get in life what we strongly determine. It is important to inquire into our innermost heart whether peace is really what we want. The inquiry into our heart is a difficult thing to do. Most people have a steel door of thick dimensions covering the opening of their heart. They can't get in to find out what's going on inside. But all of us need to try to get in as far as possible and check our priorities.

In moments of turmoil, when we are either not getting the supremacy we want or we feel really inferior, then all we desire is peace. When it all subsides again and neither the superiority nor the inferiority is very distinct, then what happens? Is it really peace we want? Or do we want to be somebody special, somebody important or lovable?

A "somebody" never has peace. There is a good story about a mango tree: a king went riding in the forest and encountered a mango tree laden with fruit. He said to

All of Us

his servants: "Go back in the evening and collect the mangoes," because he wanted them for the royal dinner table. The servants went back to the forest and returned to the palace empty-handed and told the king: "Sorry, sir, the mangoes were all gone, there wasn't a single mango left on the tree." The king thought the servants had been too lazy to go back to the forest, so he rode out himself. What he saw, instead of the beautiful mango tree laden with fruit, was a pitiful, bedraggled tree that had been beaten and robbed of its fruit and leaves. Someone, unable to reach all the branches, had broken them and had taken all the fruit. As the king rode a little farther, he came upon another mango tree, beautiful in all its green splendour, but not a single fruit on it. Nobody had gone near it, since there was no fruit, and so it was left in peace. The king went back to his palace, gave his royal crown and sceptre to his ministers and said: "You may now have the kingdom; I am going to live in a hut in the forest."

When we are nobody and have nothing, then there's no danger of warfare or attack, then there's peace. The mango tree laden with fruit didn't have a moment's peace: everybody wanted its fruit. If we really want peace, we have to be nobody—neither important, nor clever, nor beautiful, nor famous, nor right, nor in charge of anything. We need to be unobtrusive and with as few attributes as possible. The mango tree which didn't have any fruit was standing peacefully in all its splendour giving shade. To be nobody doesn't mean never to do anything again. It just means to act without self-display and without craving for results. The mango tree had shade to give, but it didn't display its wares or fret whether anyone wanted its shade. This kind of ability allows for inner peace. It is a rare ability, because most people vacillate from one extreme to another, either doing nothing and thinking, "Let them see how they get along without me," or being in charge and projecting their own views and ideas.

It seems to be so much more ingrained in us and so much more important to be "somebody," than to have peace. So we need to inquire with great care what we are truly looking for. What is it that we want out of life? If we want to be important, appreciated, loved, then we have to take their opposites in stride also. Every positive brings with it a negative, just as the sun throws shadows. If we want the one, we must accept the other, without moaning about it.

But if we really want a peaceful heart and mind, inner security and solidity, then we have to give up wanting to be somebody, anybody at all. Body and mind will not disappear because of that; what disappears is the urge and the reaching out and the affirmation of the importance and supremacy of this particular person called "me."

Every human being considers himself or herself important. There are billions of people on this globe, yet how many will mourn us? Count them for a moment. Six or eight, or twelve or fifteen, out of all these billions? This consideration may show us that we have a vastly exaggerated idea of our own importance. The more we can get that into the proper perspective, the easier life is.

Wanting to be somebody is dangerous. It's like playing with a burning fire into which we put our hands all the time and it hurts constantly. Nobody will play that game according to our own rules. People who really manage to be somebody, like heads of state, invariably need a solid bodyguard around them because they are in danger of their lives. Nobody likes to admit that someone else is more important. One of the major deterrents to peace of mind is the "somebody" of our own creation.

In the world we live in, we can find people, animals, nature and man-made things. Within all this, if we want to be in charge of anything, the only thing we have any jurisdiction over is our own heart and mind. If we really want to be somebody, we could try to be that rare person, the one who is in charge of his own heart and mind. To be somebody like that is not only very rare, but also brings with it the most beneficial results. Such a person does not fall into the trap of the defilements. Although the defilements may not be uprooted yet, he won't commit the error of displaying them and getting involved with them.

There is a story about Tan Ajahn Chah, a famous meditation master in north-east Thailand. He was accused by someone of having a lot of hatred to which Tan Ajahn Chah replied: "That may be so but I don't make any use of it." An answer like this comes from a deep understanding of our own nature, which is why we are impressed with such a reply. It's a rare person who will not allow himself to be defiled by thought, speech or action. That one is really somebody, and doesn't have to prove it to anyone else, mainly because it is quite obvious. In any case, such a person has no desire to prove anything. There's only one abiding interest and that's their own peace of mind.

When we have peace of mind as our priority, everything that is in the mind and everything that comes out in speech or action is directed towards it. Anything that does not create peace of mind is discarded, yet we must not confuse this with being right or having the last word. Others need not agree. Peace of mind is our own; all of us have to find it through our own efforts.

V. War and Peace

War and peace are the epic saga of humanity. They are all that our history books contain because they are what our hearts contain.

If you have ever read Don Quixote, you'll remember that he was fighting windmills. Everybody is doing just that, fighting windmills. Don Quixote was a figment of a writer's imagination, a character portrayed as a man who believed himself to be a great warrior. He thought that every windmill he met was an enemy and started battling with it. That's exactly what we are doing within our own hearts and that's why this story has such an everlasting appeal. It tells us about ourselves. Writers and poets whose fame has outlasted their own lifetimes have always told human beings about themselves. Mostly people don't listen, because it doesn't help when somebody else tells us what's wrong with us and few care to hear it. We have to find out for ourselves, and most people don't want to do that either.

What does it really mean to fight windmills? It means fighting nothing important or real, just imaginary enemies and battles—all quite trifling matters, which we build into something solid and formidable in our minds. We say: "I can't stand that," so we start fighting, and "I don't like him," and a battle ensues, or "I feel so unhappy," and the inner war is raging. We hardly ever know what we're so unhappy about. The weather, the food, the people, the work, the leisure, the country, anything at all will usually do it. Why does this happen to us? Because of the resistance to actually letting go and becoming what we really are, namely nothing. Nobody wants to be that.

Everybody wants to be something or somebody, even if it's only Don Quixote fighting windmills. We want to be somebody who knows and acts and will become something else, someone who has certain attributes, views, opinions and ideas. Even patently wrong views are held onto tightly, because it makes the "me" more solid. It seems negative and depressing to be nobody and have nothing. We have to find out for ourselves that it is the most exhilarating and liberating feeling we can ever have. But because we fear that windmills might attack us, we don't want to let go.

Why can't we have peace in the world? Because nobody wants to disarm. Not a single country is ready to sign a disarmament pact, which all of us bemoan. Yet have we ever looked to see whether we, ourselves, have actually disarmed? When we haven't done so, why do we wonder that nobody else is ready for it either? Nobody wants to be the first one without weapons; others might win. Does it really matter? If there is nobody there, who can be conquered? How can there be a victory over nobody? Let those who fight, win every war. All that matters is to have peace in our own heart. As long as we are resisting and rejecting and continue to find all sorts of rational excuses to keep on doing that, there will be warfare.

War manifests' externally in violence, aggression and killing. How does it reveal itself internally? We have an arsenal within us, not of guns and atomic bombs, but having the same effect, and the one who gets hurt is always the one who is shooting, namely ourselves. Sometimes another person comes within firing range and if he or she isn't careful enough, he or she is wounded. That's a regrettable accident. But the main blasts are the bombs that go off in our own heart. Where they are detonated, that's the disaster area. The arsenal we carry around within ourselves consists of our ill will and anger, our desires and cravings.

The only indicator of this internal arsenal is that we don't feel peaceful inside. We need not believe in anything; we can just look to see whether there is peace and joy in our heart. If they are lacking, most people try to find them in the world outside of themselves. That's how all wars start. It is always the other country's fault or, if one can't find anyone to blame, then one needs more *Lebensraum*, more room for expansion, more territorial sovereignty. In personal terms, we need more entertainment, more pleasure, more comfort, more distractions for the mind. If we can't find anyone else to blame for our lack of peace, then we believe it to be an unfulfilled need.

Who is that person who needs more? A figment of our own imagination? That "more" is never ending. We can go from country to country, from person to person. There are billions of people on this globe; it's hardly likely that we will want to see every one of them, or even one-hundredth; a lifetime wouldn't be enough time to do so. We may choose twenty or thirty people and then go from one to the next and back again, moving from one activity to another, from one idea to another. In reality, we are fighting against our own *dukkha* and don't want to admit

War and Peace

that the windmills in our heart are self-generated. We believe somebody put them up against us, and by moving we can escape from them.

Few people come to the final conclusion that these windmills are imaginary, that we can remove them by not endowing them with strength and importance, and that we can open our hearts without fear, then gently, gradually let go of our preconceived notions and opinions, views and ideas, suppressions and conditioned responses. When all that is removed, what do we have left? A large, open space, which we can fill with whatever we like. If we have good sense, we will fill it with love, compassion and equanimity. Then there is nothing left to fight. Only joy and peacefulness remain, which cannot be found outside of ourselves. It is quite impossible to take anything from outside and put it into ourselves. There is no opening in us through which peace can enter. We have to start within and work outward. Unless that becomes clear to us, we will always find another crusade.

Imagine what it was like in the days of the Crusades! There were those noble knights who spent all their wealth on equipping themselves with the most modern and advanced weapons, outfitting horses and followers, and then setting off to bring religion to the infidels. Many died on the way because of hardships and battles, and those who reached the end of the journey, the Holy Land, still did not get any results, only more warfare. When we look at this today, it seems utterly foolish.

Yet we do the same in our own lives. If, for instance, we wrote in our diary three or four years ago about something that upset us and we were to read it now, it might seem quite absurd. We might not even be able to remember why it was so important. We are constantly engaged in such useless activities with minor and unimportant trifles, and spend our energies trying to work them out to our ego-satisfaction. Wouldn't it be wiser to forget such mental formations and attend to what's really important? There is only one thing that's important to every being and that is a peaceful and happy heart. It cannot be bought, nor is it given away. Nobody can hand it to someone else, and it cannot be found. Ramana Maharshi, a sage in southern India, once said: "Peace and happiness are not our birthright. Whoever has attained them has done so by continual effort."

Some people have an idea that peace and happiness are synonymous with doing nothing, having no duties or responsibilities, being looked after by others. That's more about laziness. To gain peace and happiness we have to make unrelenting effort in our own heart. We can't achieve it through proliferation, by trying to get more; rather, only by wanting less—becoming emptier and emptier, until there is just open space to be filled with peace and happiness. As long as our hearts are full of likes and dislikes, how can peace and happiness find any room?

We can find peace within ourselves in any situation, any place, any circumstance, but only through effort, not through distraction. The world offers distractions and sense contacts, and they are often quite tempting. The more action there is, the more distracted the mind can be and the less we have to look at our own *dukkha*. When we have the time and opportunity to introspect, we find our inner reality different from what we imagined. Many people quickly look away again; they don't want to know about that. It's nobody's fault that there is *dukkha*. The only cure is letting go. It's really quite simple, but few people believe this to the point of trying it out.

There is a well-known simile about a monkey trap. The kind used in Asia is a wooden funnel with a small opening. Inside lies a sweet. The monkey, attracted by the sweet, puts his hand into the narrow opening and gets hold of the sweet. When he tries to draw his hand out again, he can't get his fist with the sweet through the narrow opening. He is trapped and the hunter comes and capture him. He doesn't realize that all he has to do to be free is to let go of the sweet.

That's what our life is all about—a trap—because we want it nice and sweet. Not being able to let go, we're caught in the ever-recurring happiness/unhappiness, up/down, hoping/despairing cycle. Instead of trying out for ourselves whether we could let go and be free, we resist and reject such a notion. Yet we all agree that all that matters is peace and happiness, which can only exist in a free mind and heart.

There is a lovely story from Nazrudin, a Sufi Master, who was gifted in telling absurd tales. One day, so the story goes, he sent one of his disciples to the market and asked him to buy him a bag of chillies. The disciple did as requested and brought the bag to Nazrudin, who began to eat the chillies, one after another. Soon his face turned red, his nose started running, his eyes began to water and he was choking. The disciple observed this for a while with awe and then said: "Sir, your face is turning red, your eyes are watering and you are choking. Why don't you stop eating these chillies?" Nazrudin replied: "I am waiting for a sweet one."

The teaching aid of chillies! We, too, are waiting for something, somewhere, that will create peace and happiness for us. Meanwhile there is nothing but *dukkha*, the eyes are watering, the nose is running, but we won't stop our own creations. There must be a sweet one at the bottom of the bag! It's no use thinking, hearing or reading about it; the only effective way is to look inside our own heart and see with understanding. The more the heart is full of wanting and desiring, the harder and more difficult life becomes.

Why fight all these windmills? They are self-built and can also be self-removed. It's a very rewarding experience to check what's cluttering up our own heart and mind. As we find emotion after emotion, we try not to create allowances and justifications for them, but to realize that they constitute the world's battle-grounds and start dismantling the weapons so that disarmament becomes a reality.

VI. Truth

Truth occupies a very important position in the Buddha's teaching. The Four Noble Truths are the hub of the wheel of the Dhamma. Truth (*sacca*) is one of the ten perfections to be cultivated in order to purify ourselves.

Truth can have different aspects. If we want to find an end to suffering, we have to find truth at its deepest level. The moral precepts, which include "not lying," are a basic training without which we can't lead a spiritual life.

To get to the heart of truth, we have to get to the heart of ourselves, and that is not an easy thing to do, which is further aggravated by the problem of not loving ourselves. It naturally follows that if we want to learn to love ourselves, there must also be hate present, and we are caught in this world of duality.

While we are floating around in the world of duality, we can't get to the heart of truth, because we are suspended in a wave going back and forth. There is an interesting admonition in the Sutta Nipāta which talks about not forming associates, so preventing attachments. Thus, neither love nor hate results, so that only equanimity remains, an even-mindedness towards all that exists. With equanimity we are no longer suspended between good and bad, love and hate, friend and enemy; rather, we have been able to let go, and so get to the heart of matter where truth can be found.

If we want to find the basic, underlying truth of all existence, we must practise "letting go." This includes our

All of Us

weakest and our strongest attachments, many of which aren't even recognized as clinging.

To return to the simile about truth, we can see that if we are clinging to anything, we can't get to it. We're attached to the things, people, ideas and views that we consider ours and believe to be right and useful. These attachments will keep us from getting in touch with absolute truth.

Our reactions, the likes and dislikes, hold us in suspense. While it is more pleasant to like something or someone, nevertheless both of these (likes and dislikes) are due to attachments. This difficulty is closely associated with distraction in meditation. Just as we are attached to the food that we get for the body, we are equally attached to food for the mind, so the thoughts go here and there, picking up titbits. As we do that, we are again held in suspense, moving from thought to breath and back again, being in the world of duality. When our minds are like this, it cannot get to the heart of the matter.

Understanding enables the release from suffering. When we go deeper and deeper into ourselves, one finds no core, and learns to let go of all attachments. Whether we find anything within us that is pure, desirable, commendable, or whether it's impure and unpleasant, makes no difference. All mental states owned and cherished keep us in duality, where we are hanging in mid-air, feeling very insecure. They cannot bring an end to suffering. One moment all might be well in our world and we love everyone, but five minutes later we might react with hate and rejection.

We might be able to agree with the Buddha's words or regard them as a plausible explanation, but

Truth

without the certainty of personal experience, this is of limited assistance to us. In order to have direct knowledge, it's as if we were a weight and must not be tied to anything, so that we can sink down to the bottom of all the obstructions, to see the truth shining through. The tool for that is a powerful mind, a weighty mind. As long as the mind is interested in petty concerns, it doesn't have the weightiness that can bring it to the depth of understanding.

For most of us, our minds are not in the heavy-weight class, but more akin to bantam weight. The punch of a heavy-weight really accomplishes something, whereas that of a bantam weight is not too meaningful. The light-weight mind is attached here and there to people and their opinions, to our own opinions, to the whole duality of pure and impure, right and wrong.

Why do we take things so personally, when they are truly universal? That seems to be the biggest difference between either living at ease and being able to let the mind delve into the deepest layer of truth, or living at loggerheads with ourselves and others. Neither hate nor greed is a personal manifestation; nobody has a singular claim on them, they belong to humanity. We can learn to let go of that personalized idea about our mind states, which would rid us of a serious impediment. Greed, hate and impurities exist; but by the same token non-greed and non-hate also exist. Can we own the whole lot? Or do we own them in succession or five minutes at a time for each? Why own any of them? They just exist and, seeing that, it becomes possible to let ourselves sink into the depth of the Buddha's vision.

All of Us

The deepest truth that the Buddha taught was that there is no individual person. This has to be experienced and accepted at a feeling level. As long as we haven't let go of owning body and mind, we cannot accept that we aren't really this person. This is a gradual process. In meditation we learn to let go of ideas and stories and attend to the meditation subject. If we don't let go, we cannot sink into the meditation. The mind has to be a heavy-weight for that, too.

We can compare the ordinary mind to bobbing around on the waves of thoughts and feelings. The same happens in meditation, and therefore we need to prepare ourselves for it. We can look at all mind states arising during the day and learn to let go of them. The ease and buoyancy which arises from this process is due to being unattached. If we don't practise throughout the day, our meditation suffers because we have not come to the meditation cushion in a suitable frame of mind. If we have been letting go all day, then the mind is ready and can now let go in meditation as well, thus experiencing its own happiness and purity.

Sometimes people think of the teaching as a sort of therapy, which it undoubtedly is, but that's not its ultimate aim, only one of its secondary aspects. The Buddha's teaching takes us to the end of suffering, once and for all, not just momentarily when things go wrong.

Having had an experience of letting go, even just once, proves beyond a shadow of a doubt that it means getting rid of a great burden. Carrying our hate and greed around is a heavy load, which, when abandoned, gets us out of the duality of judgment. It's pleasant to be without judgment; mental formations are troublesome.

Truth

If we succeed even once or twice during a day to let go of our reactions, we have taken a great step and can more easily do it again. We have realized that a feeling which has arisen can be stopped; it need not be carried around all day. The relief from this will be the proof that a great inner discovery has been made and that the simplicity of non-duality shows us the way towards truth.

VII. Renunciation

In order to embrace the spiritual path fully, to be able to grow on it and walk along it with a feeling of security, we have to renounce.

Renunciation doesn't necessarily mean cutting off our hair or wearing robes; rather, it means letting go of all ideas and hopes that the mind would like to grasp and retain, be interested in, and wants to investigate. The mind wants to have more of whatever is available. If it can't get more, then it makes up fantasies and imaginings, and projects them upon the world. That will never bring true satisfaction, inner peace, which can only be won by renunciation. "Letting go" is the key phrase of the Buddhist path, the fading away of desire. We must realize once and for all that "more" is not "better." It is impossible to come to an end of "more;" there is always something beyond it, but it is certainly possible to come to the end of "less," which is a much more sensible approach.

Why sit in seclusion in meditation and spoil our chances at all the opportunities the world offers for enjoyment? We could go on trips, work at a challenging job, meet interesting people, write letters or read books, have a pleasant time somewhere else and really feel at ease—we could even find a different spiritual path. When the meditation does not succeed, the thought may arise: "What am I really doing, why am I doing it, what for, what's the good of it?" Then the idea comes: "I can't really do this very well, maybe I should try something else."

Renunciation

The world glitters and promises so much, but never keeps its promises. Everyone has tried a number of its temptations and not one of them has really been fulfilling. The real fulfilment, the completeness of peace, lacking nothing, the totality of being at ease and not wanting anything, cannot be fulfilled by anything in the world. There's nothing that can fill our wants utterly and completely. Money, material possessions, another person—some of these can do so for a while, yet there's often that niggling doubt: "Maybe I'll find something else, more comfortable, easier, not so demanding and, above all, something new." Always that which is new promises fulfilment.

The mind has to be understood for what it is, just another sense, which has as its base the brain, just as seeing has as its base the eye. As the mind states arise and contact is made with them, we start believing what we are thinking and even owning it: "It's mine." Because of that, we're really interested in our thoughts and want to look after them. It's a foregone conclusion that people look after their own belongings much better than they look after other people's things, so we follow our own mind states and believe them all. Yet they will never bring lasting happiness. What they bring is hope and worry and doubt. Sometimes they supply entertainment, but, at other times, depression. When doubts arise and we follow through on them, go along with them, they can lead us to the point at which there is no practice left at all. The only way to prove that the spiritual life brings fulfilment is to practise. The proof of the pudding lies in the eating, as the saying goes. Nobody else can prove it to us. Wanting outside proof, so that all we have to do is grab hold of it and nourish ourselves, is a wrong approach.

The fulfilment we are looking for is not what we can get and stuff into this mind and body; the gaping hole is much too large to fill. The only way we can find fulfilment is to let go of expectations and wanting, of everything that goes on in the mind, so that there is no sense of any lack; then there's nothing left to fill.

The misunderstanding that recurs over and over again is this typical attitude of "I want to be given. I want to get knowledge, understanding, loving-kindness, consideration. I want to receive a spiritual awakening." There is nothing that we can be given, except instructions and methods. We need to do the daily work of practice, so that purification will result. The lack of fulfilment cannot be remedied by wanting to be given something new. We're not even clear about where this is to come from. Maybe from the Buddha, or from the Dhamma, or we might want it from our teacher. Possibly we would like to get it from our meditation, or from a book, but the answer is not in getting something from outside of ourselves; rather, it lies in discarding everything.

What do we need to get rid of first? Preferably the convolutions of the mind that constantly tell us stories which are fantastic and unbelievable, yet we believe them. One way to disbelieve them is to write them down because they seem more absurd when they're written down on paper. The mind can always think up new stories, there's no end to them. Renunciation is the key: giving up, letting go.

Giving up also means giving in to that underlying, subconscious knowing that the worldly way doesn't work, that there is a different way. We cannot try to

Renunciation

remain in the world and add something to our life; we need to give up our ambitions completely. To stay the way we are and then add something to that, how can that possibly work? If we have a non-functioning machine and add another part to it, it's not going to make it function. We have to overhaul the whole machine.

This means accepting our underlying understanding that the old ways of thinking aren't useful. There's always more *dukkha*. It keeps coming, doesn't it? Sometimes we think: "It must be due to a particular person, or maybe it's due to the weather." Then the weather changes or that person leaves, but *dukkha* is still present. So it wasn't that and we have to try to find another cause. Instead we need to become pliable and soft, and attend to that which is truly arising without all the convolutions, conglomerations, proliferations of the mind. That which arises may be either pure or impure and we need to know how to handle each one.

Once we start explaining and rationalizing, the whole process breaks down again. It is a mistake to think that we can add anything to ourselves in order to make us whole because, in fact, everything has to be taken away, the whole identifiable lot; then we become a whole person. Renunciation is letting go of ideation, of the mind-stuff that claims to be the person who knows. Who knows that person who knows? These are only ideas churning around, arising and ceasing. Renunciation is not an outward manifestation; that's only its result. The cause is an inward one, the one we need to practise. If we think of a nunnery as a place for meditation, we will find that meditation cannot happen without renunciation.

VIII. Ideal Solitude

In the Sutta Nipāta we find a discourse by the Buddha entitled "The Rhinoceros Horn" in which he compares the one horn of the rhinoceros with the sage's solitude. The Buddha praises being alone and the refrain to every stanza of the sutta is: "One should wander solitary as a rhinoceros horn."[1]

There are two kinds of solitude: that of the mind (*citta-viveka*) and that of the body (*kāya-viveka*). Everyone is familiar with solitude of the body. We go away and sit by ourselves in a room or cave, or we tell the people we are living with that we want to be left alone. People usually like that sort of solitude for short periods. If this aloneness is maintained, it is often due to people not being able to get along with others or being afraid of them because there isn't enough love in their own hearts. Often there may be a feeling of loneliness, which is detrimental to solitude, for loneliness is a negative state of mind in which we feel bereft of companionship.

When we live in a family or community, it is sometimes difficult to find physical solitude, and it's not even very practical, but physical solitude is not the only kind of aloneness there is. Mental solitude is an important factor for practice. Unless we are able to arouse mental solitude in ourselves, we will not be able to be introspective, to find out what changes in ourselves.

---

1. Transl. K.R. Norman, *Group of Discourses*; P.T.S.)

Ideal Solitude

Mental solitude means first and foremost not to be dependent on others for approval, for companionable talk, for a relationship. It doesn't mean that we become unfriendly towards others, just that we are mentally independent. If another person is kind to us, all well and good, but if that isn't the case, that's fine too, and makes no difference.

The horn of a rhinoceros is straight and solid and so strong that we can't bend it. Can our minds be like that? Mental solitude cuts out idle chatter—talking about nothing at all, just letting off steam—which is detrimental to spiritual growth. When we let the steam go from a pot, we can't cook the food. Our practice can be likened to putting the heat on ourselves. If we let off steam again and again, that inner process is stopped. It's much better to let the steam accumulate and find out what is cooking. That is the most important work we can do.

Everybody should have occasion each day to be on her own physically for some time, so that we can really feel alone, totally by ourselves. Sometimes we may think: "People are talking about me." That doesn't matter; we are the owners of our own *kamma*. If somebody talks about us, it's their *kamma*. If we get upset, that's our *kamma*. Getting interested in what is being said is enough to show that we are dependent on people's approval. Who's approving of whom? Maybe the five *khandhas* (body, feeling, perception, mental formations and consciousness) are approving, or possibly the hair of the head, or of the body, or the nails, teeth, skin? Which 'self' is approving, the good one, the bad one, the mediocre one, or maybe the non-self?

All of Us

Unless we can find a feeling of solidity in ourselves, from the centre, where there is no movement, we are always going to feel insecure. Nobody can be liked by everyone, not even the Buddha. Because we have defilements, we are always on the lookout for everybody else's pollutions. None of that matters; it's all totally unimportant. The only thing that is significant is to be mindful—totally attentive to each step on the way, to what we are doing, feeling, thinking. It's so easy to forget this. There's always somebody with whom to talk or another cup of tea to be had. That's how the world lives and the inhabitants are mostly unhappy, but the Buddha's path leads out of the world to independent happiness.

Letting off steam, idle chatter and looking for companionship are unskilful things to do. Trying to find out what people are thinking about us, is immaterial and irrelevant and has nothing to do with the spiritual path. Solitude in the mind means that we can be alone in the midst of the crowd. Even in a large and agitated crowd of people, we would still be able to operate from our own centre, giving out love and compassion, and not being influenced by what is happening around us.

That can be called ideal solitude and means we have removed ourselves from the future and past, which is necessary in order to stand straight and alone. If we are attached to the future, then there is worry, and if we are hankering for the past, there is either desire or rejection, both of which represent the constant chatter of the mind, not conducive to mental solitude.

Solitude can only be fully experienced when there is inner peace. Otherwise loneliness pushes us to try and remedy the feeling of emptiness and loss. "Where is everybody? What can I do without some companionship? I must discuss my problems." Mindfulness is able to take care of all that because it arises in the present moment and has nothing to do with the future or the past. It keeps us totally occupied and saves us from making mistakes which are natural to human beings: the greater the mindfulness, the fewer the mistakes. Errors on the mundane level also have repercussions on the supramundane path, because they are due to a lack of mindfulness, which does not allow us to get past our self-inflicted *dukkha*. We will try again and again to find someone who is to blame, or someone who can distract us.

Ideal solitude arises when a person can be alone or with others and remain unaffected, not getting caught in someone else's difficulties. We may respond in an appropriate manner, but we are not affected. We all have our own inner life and we only get to know it well when the mind stops chattering and we can attend to our inner feelings. Once we have seen what is happening inside of us, we will want to change it. Only the fully Enlightened One (*Arahant*) has an inner life which needs no changing. Our inner stress and lack of peace push us outward to find someone who will remove a moment of *dukkha*, but only we, ourselves, can do it.

Solitude may be physical, but that's not its main function. The solitary mind is one which can have profound and original thoughts. A dependent mind thinks in clichés, the way everybody else does, because it wants approval. Such a mind understands at a surface level, just like the world does, and cannot grasp the profundity and depth of the Buddha's teaching. The solitary mind is at ease because it is unaffected.

All of Us

It's interesting that a mind at ease, which can stand on its own, can also memorize easily because such a mind is not filled with the desire to remove *dukkha*. It can remember without much trouble. This is one of its side benefits, but the main value of a solitary mind is its imperturbability. It can't be shaken and will stand without support, just as a strong tree doesn't need a prop because it is powerful in its own right. If the mind doesn't have enough vigour to stand on its own, it won't have the strength and determination to fulfil the Dhamma.

Our practice includes being on our own some of the time each day to introspect and contemplate. Reading, talking and listening are all communication with others, which are necessary at times, but it is essential to have time for the self-inquiry that asks: "What is happening within me? What am I feeling? Is it wholesome or not? Am I perfectly contented on my own? How much self-concern is there? Is the Dhamma my guide or am I bewildered?" If there's a fog in our mind, all we need is a searchlight to penetrate it, and that searchlight is concentration.

Health, wealth and youth do not mean there will be no *dukkha*. They are a cover-up. Ill health, poverty and old age make it easier to realize the unsatisfactoriness of our existence. When we are alone, that is the time to get to know ourselves. We can investigate the meaning of the Dhamma we've heard and whether we can actualize it in our own lives, and we can use those aspects of the Dhamma that are most meaningful for us.

The solitary mind is a strong mind because it knows how to stand still. This doesn't mean not associating with people at all; that would lack loving-kindness (*mettā*). A solitary mind is able to be alone and introspect and also be loving towards others. Living in a Dhamma community is an ideal place to practise this.

Meditation is the means for concentration, the tool to break through the fog enveloping everyone who is not an Arahant. At times, in communal living, there is togetherness and lovingness and service. These should be the results of *mettā*, not of trying to get away from *dukkha*. Next time we start a conversation, let's first investigate: "Why am I having this discussion? Is it necessary, or am I bored and want to get away from my problems."

Clear comprehension is the mental factor which joins with mindfulness to give purpose and direction. We examine whether our speech and actions are having the right purpose, whether we are using skilful means and whether the initial purpose has been accomplished. If we have no clear-cut direction, idle chatter results. Even in meditation the mind does it, which is due to lack of training. When we practise clear comprehension, we need to stop a moment and examine the whole situation before plunging in. This may become one of our skilful habits, not often found in the world.

An important aspect of the Buddha's teaching is the combination of clear comprehension with mindfulness. The Buddha often recommends them as the way out of all sorrow, and we need to practise them in our small, everyday efforts. This may consist of learning something new, a Dhamma sentence remembered, one line of chanting memorized, one new insight about ourselves, one aspect of reality realized. Such a mind gains strength and self-confidence.

Renunciation is the greatest help in gaining self-confidence. We know we can get along without practically everything, for instance food, for quite some time. Once the Buddha went to a village where nobody had any faith in him. He received no alms-food at all; nobody in the village paid any attention to him. He went to the outskirts and sat down on a bit of straw and meditated. Another ascetic came by who had seen that the Buddha had not received any food and commiserated with him: "You must be feeling very badly not having anything to eat. I'm very sorry. You don't even have a nice place to sleep, just straw." The Buddha replied: "Feeders on joy we are. Inner joy can feed us for many days."

We can get along without many things when they are voluntarily given up. If someone takes our belongings, we resist, which is *dukkha*. But when we practise self-denial, we gain strength and enable the mind to stand on its own. Self-confidence arises and creates a really strong backbone. Renunciation of companionship shows us whether we are self-sufficient.

The Buddha did not advocate exaggerated and harmful ascetic practices, but we could give up, for instance, afternoon conversations and contemplate instead. Afterwards the mind feels contented with its own efforts. The more effort we can make, the more satisfaction arises.

We need a solitary mind in meditation, so we need to practise it some time during each day. The secluded mind has two attributes: one is mindfulness, full attention and clear comprehension; and the other is introspection and contemplation. Both of them bring the mind to unification. Only in togetherness lies strength; unification brings power.

IX. DUKKHA FOR KNOWLEDGE AND VISION

The twelve-point "dependent origination" (*paṭiccasamuppāda*) starts with ignorance (*avijjā*) and goes through *kamma* formations (*saṅkhārā*), rebirth consciousness, mind and matter, sense contacts, feeling, craving, clinging, becoming, birth, and ends with death. Getting born means dying. During that sequence there is one point of escape—between feeling and craving.

While this is called the mundane (*lokiya*) dependent-origination, the Buddha also taught a supramundane, transcendental (*lokuttara*) series of cause and effect, which starts with unsatisfactoriness, *dukkha*. *Dukkha* needs to be seen for what it really is, namely the best starting point for our spiritual journey. Unless we know and see *dukkha*, we would have little reason to practise. If we haven't acknowledged the overall existence of *dukkha*, we wouldn't be interested in getting out of its clutches.

The transcendental dependent-origination starts out with the awareness and inner knowledge of the inescapable suffering in the human realm. When we reflect upon this, we will no longer try to find a way out through human endeavour, nor through becoming more informed or knowledgeable, or richer, or owning more, or having more friends. Seeing *dukkha* as an inescapable condition, bound up with existence, we no longer feel oppressed by it. It is inescapable that there is thunder and lightning and rain; we don't try to reject the weather. There has to be thunder, lightning and rain so we can grow food.

Dukkha is equally inescapable. Without it, the human condition would not exist; there wouldn't be rebirth, decay and death. Seeing it like that, we lose our resistance to it. The moment we are no longer repelled by *dukkha*, suffering is greatly diminished. It's our resistance that creates the craving to get rid of it, which makes it so much worse.

Having understood *dukkha* in this way, we may be fortunate enough to make contact with the true Dhamma, the Buddha's teaching, which is then due to our own good *kamma*. There are innumerable people who never get in touch with Dhamma. They might even be born in a place where the Dhamma is being preached, but they will have no opportunity to hear it. There are many more people who will not be searching for the Dhamma, because they're still searching for the escape route in the human endeavour, but looking in the wrong direction. Having come to the conclusion that the world will not provide real or lasting happiness, we also have to have the good *kamma* to be able to listen to true Dhamma. If these conditions arise, then faith results.

Faith has to be based on trust and confidence. If these are lacking, the path will not be revealed. We become trusting like a child holding the hand of a grown-up when crossing the street, believing that the grown-up will take care of it by watching out for traffic so that no accident happens. The small child doesn't have the capacity to gauge when it's safe to cross but trusts in someone with greater experience.

We are like children compared to the Buddha. If we can have a child-like innocence, then it will be possible for

Dukkha for Knowledge and Vision

us to give ourselves unstintingly to the teaching and the practice, holding onto the hand of the true Dhamma that will guide us. Life and practice will be simplified when the judging and considering is removed. No longer will we question: "I should do it another way, or go somewhere else, or find out how it is done by others." These are possibilities, but they are not conducive to good practice or to getting out of *dukkha*. Trust in the Dhamma helps to keep the mind steady. We have to find out for ourselves if this is the correct escape route, but if we don't try, we won't know.

If *dukkha* is still regarded as a calamity, we will not have enough space in the mind to have trust. The mind will be full of grief, pain, lamentation, forgetting that all of us are experiencing the result of our *kamma* and nothing else. This is part of being a human being, subject to our own *kamma*.

Resistance to *dukkha* saps our energy and the mind cannot stretch to its full capacity. If *dukkha* is seen as the necessary ingredient to spur us on to leave *saṃsāra* behind, then our positive attitude will point in the right direction. *Dukkha* is not a tragedy, but rather a basic ingredient for insight. This must not only be a thinking process, but it must also be felt with our heart. It's too easy to think like that and not to do anything about it. But when our heart is truly touched, trust and confidence in the Dhamma arise as the way out of all suffering.

The Dhamma is totally opposed to worldly thinking, where suffering is considered to be a great misfortune. In the Dhamma, suffering is seen as the first step to transcend the human condition. The understanding of *dukkha* has to be solid in order to arouse

All of Us

trust in that part of the teaching which we haven't experienced ourselves yet. If we have already tried many other escape routes and none of them actually worked, then we will find it easier to become that trusting childlike person, walking along this difficult path without turning right or left, knowing that the teaching is true, and letting it be our guide. Such faith brings joy, without which the path is a heavy burden and will not flourish. Joy is a necessary and essential ingredient of the spiritual life.

Joy is not to be mistaken for pleasure, exhilaration or exuberance. Joy is a feeling of ease and gladness, knowing we have found that which transcends all suffering. People sometimes have the mistaken idea that to be holy or pious means having a sad face and walking around in a mournful way. Yet the Buddha is said never to have cried and is usually depicted with a half-smile on his face. Holiness does not stand for sadness: it means wholeness. Without joy there is no wholeness. This inner joy carries with it the certainty that the path is blameless, the practice is fruitful, and the conduct is appropriate.

We need to sit down for meditation with a joyous feeling and the whole experience of meditation will culminate in happiness. This brings us tranquillity, as we no longer look around for outside satisfaction. We know only to look into ourselves. There's nowhere to go and nothing to do; it's all happening within. Such tranquillity is helpful to focused meditation and creates the feeling of being in the right spot at the right time. It also creates ease of mind, which facilitates meditation and is conducive to eliminating sceptical doubt (*vicikicchā*).

Sceptical doubt is the harbinger of restlessness, whereas joy begets calm. We need not worry about our

Dukkha for Knowledge and Vision

own or the world's future; it's just a matter of time until we fathom absolute reality. When the path, practice and effort mesh together, results are bound to come. It is essential to have complete confidence in everything the Buddha said. We can't pick out the ideas we want to believe because they happen to be in accordance with what we like anyway, and discard others. There are no choices to be made; it's all or nothing.

Tranquillity helps concentration to arise. *Dukkha* itself can lead us to proper concentration if we handle it properly. We mustn't reject it, thinking that it is a quirk of fate that has brought us all this grief, or thinking that other people are causing it. Instead, if we use *dukkha* to push us onto the path, then proper concentration can result.

Right concentration makes it possible for the mind to stretch. The mind that is limited, obstructed and defiled cannot grasp the profundity of the teachings. It may get an inkling that there is something extraordinary available, but it cannot go into the depth of it. Only the focused mind can extend beyond its limitations, and when it does that, it may experience the "knowledge and vision of things as they really are."

The Buddha often used this phrase "knowledge and vision of things as they really are" (*yathābhūtañāṇadassana*). This is distinct from the way we think things are, or might be, or as we'd like them to be—usually comfortable and pleasant. Instead we have birth, decay, disease and death, not getting what we want, or getting what we don't want—a constant perception of what we dislike, which fails to support our ego-belief. In knowing and seeing things as they really are, we will lose this distaste.

All of Us

We will come to see that within this realm of impermanence, unsatisfactoriness and corelessness (*anicca, dukkha, anattā*), there is nothing that can be grasped and found to be solid and satisfying. No person, no possession, no thought, no feeling. Nothing can be clung to and found to be steady and supportive.

This is what is called right view, beyond our ordinary everyday perception and results from right concentration, which comes from dealing with *dukkha* in a positive, welcoming way. When we try to escape from *dukkha* by forgetting about it, or running away from it, or blaming someone else, or becoming depressed by it, or feeling sorry for ourselves, we are creating more *dukkha*. All these methods are based on self-delusion. The "knowledge and vision of things as they really are" is the first step on the noble path; everything else has been the preliminary work.

Sometimes our understanding may feel like one of those mystery pictures that children play with. Now you see it, now you don't. When any aspect of Dhamma is clearly visible to us, we must keep on resurrecting that vision. If it is correct, *dukkha* has no sting; it just is. Decay, disease and death do not appear fearful. There is nothing to fear, because everything falls apart continually. This body disintegrates and the mind changes every moment.

Without knowledge and vision of reality, the practice is difficult, but after having this clear perception, the practice becomes the only possible thing to do, and everything else is only a distraction. From the 'knowledge-and-vision' arises disenchantment with what the world has to offer. All the glitter that seems to be gold turns out to be fool's gold, which therefore cannot satisfy in the long term—it can give us pleasure for one moment and displeasure the next, and the pleasure has to be searched for again and again. The world of the senses has fooled us so often that we're still enmeshed in it and still experiencing *dukkha*, unless the true vision arises.

There's a poster available in Australia which reads: "Life—be in it!" Wouldn't it be better if it said, "Life—be out of it?" Life and existence are bound up with the constant renewal of our sense contacts: seeing, hearing, tasting, touching, smelling and thinking. Only when we have clear perception will disenchantment set in and we will no longer be fooled by the most wonderful sense contact—it exists, but doesn't touch our heart. Māra, the tempter, has lost his grip and has been shown the door. He's waiting at the doorstep to slip in again, at the first possible opportunity, but he isn't so comfortably ensconced inside any more.

This brings a great deal of security and satisfaction to the heart. We won't be swayed to leave this path of practice. When Māra is still calling, there's no peace in the heart. We can't be at ease and satisfied, because there's always something new to tempt us. With "knowledge and vision of things as they really are," and subsequent disenchantment, we realize that only the Buddha's path leads us to tranquillity, peace and the end of *dukkha*.

Therefore, *dukkha* is really our staunchest friend, our most faithful supporter. We'll never find another friend or helpmate like it, if it is seen in the right way, without resistance or rejection. When we use *dukkha* as our incentive for practice, gratitude and appreciation for it will arise. This takes the sting out of our pain and transforms it into our most valuable experience.

X. Our Underlying Tendencies

Most people are inclined to blame either themselves or others for whatever they consider wrong. Neither way is profitable, nor will it bring peace of mind. To really get a grip on the facts that prevail within each human being, it may help by knowing the underlying tendencies (*anusayā*) within us.

If we understand that every human being has these tendencies, then we may be less inclined to blame or be upset or take offence, and more inclined to accept things with equanimity. We may be more prone to work on these tendencies when we become aware of them in ourselves.

The underlying tendencies are more subtle than the five hindrances (*pañca nīvaraṇā*), which are gross and exhibit themselves as:

1. Sensual desire: wanting that which is pleasing to the senses.

2. Ill will: getting angry, upset.

3. Sloth and torpor: having no energy whatsoever (sloth refers to the body, torpor to the mind).

4. Restlessness and worry: being ill-at-ease, no peacefulness.

5. Sceptical doubt: not knowing which way to turn.

These five hindrances are easily discernible in ourselves and in others, but the underlying tendencies are more difficult to pinpoint. They are the hidden sources for the hindrances to arise, and in order to get rid of them, we

Our Underlying Tendencies

need keen mindfulness and a great deal of discernment.

Having worked with the five hindrances in ourselves and to a certain degree having let go of their grossest aspects, we can begin work on the underlying tendencies. The word itself suggests their characteristic, namely, that their roots are deeply imbedded and therefore hard to see and eliminate.

The first two tendencies are similar to the hindrances of sensuality and irritation, being the underlying bases for sensual desire and anger. Even when sensual desire has been largely abandoned and anger no longer arises, the disposition to sensuality and irritation remain.

Sensuality is part and parcel of a human being and shows itself in becoming attached and reacting to what we see, hear, smell, taste, touch, and think. We are concerned with what we feel and have not yet come to the understanding that the sense objects are only impermanent phenomena arising and passing away. When this lack of profound insight is still prevalent, we ascribe importance to the impressions that come in through the senses. We are drawn to them and seek pleasure in them. When the senses are still playing an important part in a person, there is sensuality. The human being is a sensuous being. There is a verse which describes the noble Sangha as having "pacified senses." The Loving-Kindness Sutta (Karaṇīyametta Sutta) describes the ideal monk as "with senses calmed." In many suttas the Buddha says that getting rid of sense desire is the way to Nibbāna.

Sensuality, as an ingrained part of being human, has to be transcended with great effort and cannot be done

All of Us

without insight. It is impossible to succeed just by avowing: "Sensuality isn't useful; I'll let go of it." We have to gain the insight that these sense contacts have no intrinsic value in themselves. There is a coming together of the sense base (eye, ear, nose, tongue, skin, mind) with the sense object (sight, sound, smell, taste, touch, thought) and the sense consciousness (seeing, hearing, smelling, tasting, touching, thinking) to form an impingement. That's all that's happening. As long as we react to these contacts as if they had importance, there is sensuality, and where there is sensuality, there is also irritation. The two go hand in hand. Sensuality is satisfied when the sense contact impingement was pleasant, and irritation arises when the sense contact was unpleasant. It doesn't have to issue as anger, shouting, fury, hate or even resistance. It is just irritation, which results in being displeased, feeling ill at ease and restless. It goes together with being a sensual human being.

Sensuality and irritation only disappear for the Non-Returner (*anāgāmī*), the last stage before full Enlightenment: one who does not return to this realm, but attains Nibbāna in the "Pure Abodes." Even the Stream-Enterer (*sotāpanna*) and the Once-Returner (*sakadāgāmi*), the first and second stages of noble attainment, are still beset by the *dukkha* of sensuality and irritation.

If we imagine that the impulse creating sensuality or irritation is outside of ourselves, we haven't seen the beginning of the path yet. It is necessary to realize that the reaction is our own, so that we may start to work on ourselves. If we don't even notice it happening, how can we do anything about it? It's occurring constantly, without let-up. We have innumerable occasions to become aware of it in our inner world.

Our Underlying Tendencies

Unfortunately becoming aware doesn't mean that we can get rid of our reactions. There also has to be an understanding of the futility of an unwholesome response, and an effort made to investigate the causes. It's easy to see that sensuality and irritation are the underlying tendencies that create sensual desire and ill will. This insight should arouse a little acceptance and tolerance towards our own difficulties and those of other people. If this is happening to everyone constantly, then what is there to get upset about? The only thing to do is to work with it, to use it as our subject for contemplation (*kammaṭṭhāna*) and introspection. It is well worthwhile to use our difficulties as our method for the task of purification.

It is as well to remember that our tendencies and hindrances are all interconnected. If we are able to diminish one, the others also become a little less obstructive; they lose their heaviness and cease to be so frightening. People generally fear their own reactions. That is why they often feel threatened by others; they're not so much afraid of the other person's reaction, but far more so of their own. They're unsure of themselves, fearing to become aggressive, angry, and then losing some of their own self-image.

Having a self-image is very detrimental, because it is based on the illusion of permanence. Everything constantly changes, including ourselves, while a self-image presupposes stability. One moment we may be a sensual being, the next moment an irritable one. Sometimes we are at ease, at other times we are restless. Which one are we? To have an image of ourselves creates a concept of permanence which can never have any basis in fact. It blocks our insight into the underlying tendencies because we will be blind to those which do not fit our image.

The third underlying tendency is doubt or hesitation. If we have doubts, we hesitate: "What am I going to do next?" We doubt our own path and abilities, and how to proceed. Due to hesitation, we don't use our time wisely. At times we may waste it or over-indulge in activities that are not beneficial. Doubt means that we don't have an inner vision to guide us, but are obsessed by uncertainty. Doubts and hesitation lie in our hearts because of a feeling of insecurity. We are afraid of not being safe. But there's no safety anywhere; the only one that can be found is Nibbāna. This fear and insecurity in the heart cause doubt and hesitation to arise. If we were to leave them behind and not pay any attention to them, we could step ahead so much more easily and could accomplish many things.

Doubt and hesitation are abandoned with Stream-entry. One who has attained the first Path and Fruit no longer has doubts, because that person has had a personal experience of an unconditioned reality, totally different from the relative reality in which we live, and can now forge ahead without worry or fear. There can be no doubt about a direct experience. If we tell a small child: "Please don't touch the stove, you might get burned," it's quite likely that the child will nevertheless touch the stove. Having once touched it and experienced the painful feeling of being burned, the child will surely never touch it again. The experience removes doubt and hesitation.

The fourth underlying tendency is the wrong view (diṭṭhi) of relating all that happens to a "self." This goes on

Our Underlying Tendencies

constantly and we can verify that easily, as it happens to everybody. Very few people realize: "This is just mental phenomena;" they believe: "I think." When there is pain in the body, few people say: "It's just an unpleasant feeling;" instead they might say: "I'm feeling awful," or "I have a terrible pain." This reaction to whatever happens as "self" is due to an underlying tendency so deeply imbedded that it takes great effort to loosen its hold.

To lose the wrong view of self does not simply mean to understand intellectually that there is no real "self." What is required is an inner view of this whole conglomeration of mind and body as nothing but mere phenomena without ownership. The first step is taken at Stream-entry, when right view of "self" arises, though all clinging to self-concepts is abandoned only at Arahant level.

Next comes pride and conceit (*māna*), which here means having a certain concept of ourselves, such as being a man or a woman, young or old, beautiful or ugly. We conceive what we want, feel, think, know, own, and what we can do. All this conceptualizing creates ownership and we become proud of possessions, knowledge, skills, feelings, being someone special. This pride may be deeply hidden in ourselves and hard to find and may need some introspective digging. This is due to the fact that so much of our whole being is involved. When we say: "Now find that concept about being a woman," the answer often is: "Of course, I'm a woman, what else would I be?" But as long as "I am" anything—woman, man, child, stupid or intelligent—"I am" far from Nibbāna. Whatever I conceptualize myself to be stops me in my tracks.

All of Us

The underlying tendency of pride and conceit is only uprooted by the Arahant. There's no directly discernible relationship to any of the hindrances there, but the conceiving of "self" and the wrong view of "self" are the chief manifestations of delusion, the root cause for all our defilements.

Next we come to clinging to existence (*bhavarāga*). That's our survival syndrome, clinging to being here, not willing to give up, not ready to die today. We must learn to be ready to die now; not wishing to die, but to be ready for it. Wishing to die is the other side of the same coin of clinging to existence; it's trying to get rid of existence because life is too difficult. But being ready to die now means that the clinging to being someone, and being here to prove it, has been abandoned, for it has been seen to be a delusion. At this point, wrong view of "self" has been eliminated.

Clinging to existence brings us into a dependency syndrome. We want everything to work out well for us and we resent it if that doesn't happen. This creates irritation and sensuality. We mostly forget that we are only guests here on this planet and our visit is limited and can be over at any time. This clinging to being alive brings much difficulty to all of us because it projects us into the future, preventing us from attending to the present. If we don't live in the present, we're missing out on being alive at all. There's no life in the future; it's all ideation, conjecture, a hope and a prayer. If we really want to be alive and experience things as they are, we've got to be here now, attending to each moment. This entails letting go of clinging to what will happen to us in the future, particularly whether we are going to continue to exist.

Our Underlying Tendencies

Existing in this moment is enough. To be able to let go of that clinging means to let go of the future. Only then will there be strong mindfulness, real attention and clear knowing.

Clinging to existence will always give us the idea that something better will come along if we just wait long enough, and that denies effort, effort which can only be made now. Who knows what tomorrow will bring?

The last of the seven tendencies is ignorance (*avijjā*)—ignoring the Four Noble Truths. Ignorance is the so-called starting point in the chain of cause and effect which brings us back to birth and death again and again. Ignorance opposes wisdom, and here it concerns the fact that we disregard reality, not realizing that all our *dukkha* comes from wanting, even if our desire may be a wholesome one. If we continue to ignore the first two noble truths, not to speak of the third truth, which is Nibbāna, we are enmeshed in *dukkha*. Our underlying tendency of ignorance eventuates in the wrong view of "self"—the conceiving of a "self"—showing us the interconnection of all the underlying tendencies. Without ignorance there wouldn't be any sensuality and irritation, nor any hesitation or doubt, no wrong view, nor pride and conceit, no clinging to existence.

It's very useful to pick the characteristic that creates difficulties for us over and over again and make it our focus of attention. Since they are all interconnected, minimizing one will help to reduce the others to more manageable proportions.

To see these underlying tendencies in ourselves takes a great deal of proper attention towards ourselves, which needs time and solitude. We can't do it while talking with others. If the mind is clear we can do it during meditation sessions or through contemplation.

Contemplation is a valid adjunct to meditation, an important helpmate, and is always directed towards insight, while meditation may at times be geared towards serenity. Contemplation means looking inward and trying to see what arises: "What makes me tick?" With utter truthfulness, remembering the underlying tendencies, knowing that everybody has them, we can ask: "How are they manifesting in me?" Once that has been seen, there is further validity in contemplating: "What can I do about getting rid of this particular tendency, or at least minimizing it?" We should allot some time during each day for contemplation. If we have spent a whole day without introspection, we can't hope to go inward during our meditation time.

Meditation and contemplation complement and need each other.

XI. SORROWLESS, STAINLESS AND SECURE

Sorrowless, stainless and secure are three attributes of an Enlightened One (*Arahant*): sorrowless meaning no *dukkha*; stainless as in having no defilements; and secure as in having no fear. Obviously these three are extremely desirable, as they make for happiness. When we think that they are characteristics of an Arahant, we might wonder: "This is so far removed from me, how can I ever aspire to that?" The conviction might arise that it's too immense to consider for our own achievement.

We all know what it means to have sorrow (*dukkha*). We are familiar with our defilements, when we get upset, worried, anxious, envious or jealous. We all experience fear.—it can be fear of death of ourselves or of loved ones, or fear of not being liked, praised, accepted, or fear of not reaching our goals, or of making a fool of ourselves.

We also experience the opposites of those three states. The seeds are within us, otherwise Enlightenment would be a myth. It is possible to have moments of being sorrowless, stainless and secure. If we have a really focused meditation, momentarily *dukkha* doesn't arise; only one-pointedness is present. No defilements can enter because the mind is otherwise occupied. The mind can either have defilements or be focused, which is wonderful, even though this may last only a single moment. There can be no fear because all is well at such a time. The more often we regenerate these moments of being sorrowless, stainless and secure, the more they become part of ourselves and we can revert to them again.

Remembering that it is possible to do this, and bringing up these feelings, eventually this state of mind becomes more a part of a person's make-up. Just as a person who worries about not being accepted, or who worries about achieving, or lacks self-confidence, will always act accordingly. When we remember our fears, we simply re-enact them; and so the same goes for the liberated mind-states.

Every moment of concentration during meditation is a moment of no defilements, no sorrow and no fear, and this experience must be duplicated over and over again. Thereby we reinforce our liberated mind-states; as we remember them, we can retain them and act in accordance with them, even under ordinary or trying circumstances. Defilements need not arise constantly; there are pauses when there is no ill will, only loving-kindness (*mettā*); no sensual desire, only generosity and renunciation.

Sensual desire means wanting, and renunciation means giving up. When we give, we aren't desiring, unless we are wishing for applause or gratitude. If we give for giving's sake, then there is a moment of no defilement. The same holds true for loving-kindness, compassion and helpfulness, which are all opposed to greed.

When we have no doubt, being absolutely sure of what we're doing—and these moments do arise—that too is an instance of being stainless. No worries and no restlessness also add to our freedom. Not wanting to go anywhere or do anything; not worrying about what was done or left undone in the past, which is absurd anyway, when we realize that nobody will care in a year or even a month from now, least of all ourselves.

We all know moments without all this *dukkha*. When those moments arise, we are "stainless," without any blemishes, sorrowless and fearless. We feel at ease and secure. Such times are difficult to find in the world. There are so many dangers threatening our desire for survival, and they are constantly with us, but when heart and mind are fully occupied with purified states, fear does not have a chance to arise.

On our way to the "deathless," we need to regenerate these liberated moments and bring them up over and over again. We can relish these mind states, enjoying the knowledge that they are possible. It is a natural tendency to resurrect our moments of freedom again and again, so that we stay on the path to liberation.

Concentration in meditation brings a quiet and joy with it which prove with absolute certainty that they have nothing to do with outer conditions. They are strictly factors of the mind, which are our doorway to freedom. We cannot cultivate them successfully if we neglect them during those hours when we're not meditating; we need to guard and protect the mind from unwholesome thoughts at all times.

When we do experience liberated mind states, we must not think they have come to us from outside. Just as we cannot blame the external trigger for what goes wrong in the mind, so we cannot praise it for the opposite. Outside occurrences are quite unreliable and beyond our control. To depend on anything so unreliable is foolishness. Our practice is to generate the undefiled states in our minds, which opens the way to successful meditation and is the pathway to liberation. When the mind is without defilements, clear and at ease, without the convolutions of discursive thinking, simply aware, happiness and peace arise. These moments, though short-lived, are like a light at the end of a tunnel that appears dark and suffocating, seemingly never ending because, for the lack of light, we cannot see its length. If we cultivate and make much of these single moments, then there is an illumination and we can see that the tunnel does have an end, as a result of which joy is generated in our heart, and this is an important adjunct to practice.

The Buddha taught a balanced path, namely to see reality for what it is, to know that *dukkha* is inescapable, but with the counterbalance of joy from knowing that there is a way out. If we are too imbued with sorrow and are feeling weighed down under that, believing only that to be the path, then our actions and reactions will be based on our suffering. Being oppressed with *dukkha* does not make for successful meditation, nor for harmonious living. If we try to negate *dukkha*, and suppress it, then we are not facing reality. But if we see *dukkha* as a universal characteristic, knowing we can do something about its abandonment, then we are keeping in balance. We need equipoise in order to practise successfully.

XII. Path and Fruit

To have an ambition seems to be a natural phenomenon in the human make-up. Some people want to be rich, powerful or famous; others want to be very knowledgeable, and get degrees; some just want to find a little niche for themselves where they can look out the window and see the same scenery every day; and others want to find a perfect partner, or one as near perfect as possible.

Even when we are not living in the world but in a nunnery, we have ambitions: to become excellent meditators, to be perfectly peaceful, that this lifestyle should yield results. There's always something we hope for. Why is that? Because it's in the future, never in the present.

Instead of being attentive to what is now, we are hoping for something better to happen, maybe tomorrow. Then, when tomorrow arrives, it has to be the next day again, because it still wasn't perfect enough. If we were to change this pattern in our thinking habits and become more attentive to what is, then we would find something to satisfy us, but when we are looking at that which doesn't exist yet—that more perfect, more wonderful, more satisfying thing—then we can't find anything at all, because we are looking for that which isn't there.

The Buddha spoke about two kinds of people: the ordinary worldling (*puthujjana*) and the noble person (*ariya*). Obviously it is a worthwhile ambition to become a noble person, but if we keep looking for it as something that will happen in some future time, then it will escape us.

The difference between a noble one and a worldling is the experience of "path and fruit" (*magga-phala*). The first moment of this supramundane consciousness is termed Stream-entry (*sotāpatti*) and the person who experiences it is a Stream-enterer (*sotāpanna*). If we put that into our minds as a goal in the future, it will not come about, because we are not using all our energy and strength to recognize each moment. Only in the recognition of each moment can a path-moment occur.

The distinguishing factor between a worldling and a noble one is the elimination of the first three fetters binding us to continuous existence, which are: wrong view of self, sceptical doubt, and belief in rites and rituals (*sakkāyadiṭṭhi*, *vicikicchā* and *sīlabbataparāmāsa* in Pali). Anyone who is not a Stream-enterer is chained to these three wrong beliefs and reactions that lead away from freedom and bondage.

Let's take a look at sceptical doubt first. It's that niggling thought in the back of the mind: "There must be an easier way," or "I'm sure I can find happiness somewhere in this wide world." As long as there's doubt that the path of liberation leads out of the world, and the belief is there that satisfaction can be found within the world, there is no chance of noble attainment, because we are looking in the wrong direction. In this world of people and things, animals and possessions, scenery and sense contacts, there is nothing to be found other than that which we already know. If there was, why isn't it easily discernible, then, and why haven't we found it yet? It should be quite plain to see. So what are we looking for?

Path and Fruit

Obviously we are looking for happiness and peace, like everyone else. Sceptical doubt, that alarmist, says: "I'm sure if I just handled things a bit more cleverly than I did last time I'd be happy. There are a few things I haven't tried yet." Maybe we haven't flown our own plane yet, or lived in a cave in the Himalayas, or sailed around the world, or written that best-selling novel. All of these are splendid things to do in the world, except they are a waste of time and energy if true freedom is what you are seeking.

Sceptical doubt makes itself felt when we aren't quite sure what our next move should be. "Where am I going, what am I to do?" We haven't found a direction yet. Sceptical doubt is the fetter in the mind when the clarity which comes from a path-moment is absent. When the clarity which comes from a path-moment is present, the consciousness arising at that time removes all doubt, because we have experienced the proof ourselves. When we bite into the mango, for example, we know its taste.

The wrong view of self is the most damaging fetter that besets the ordinary person. It contains the deeply imbedded 'this is me' notion. There is this 'someone' who is meditating. This 'someone' wants to get enlightened, wants to become a Stream-enterer, wants to be happy. This wrong view of self is the cause of all problems that could possibly arise.

As long as there's 'somebody' there, that person can have problems. When there's nobody there, who can have difficulties? Wrong view of self is the root that generates all subsequent pain, grief and lamentation. With it also come the fears and worries: "Am I going to be all right, happy, peaceful, find what I am looking for, get what I want, be healthy, wealthy and wise?" These worries and fears are well substantiated from our own past. We haven't always been healthy, wealthy and wise, or received what we wanted, nor felt wonderful. So there's a very good reason to be worried and fearful as long as wrong view of self prevails.

Rites and rituals in themselves are not harmful, but believing them to be part of the path to Nibbāna is detrimental. They need not even be religious ones, though we usually think of them like that, such as offering flowers and incense on a shrine, prostrating or celebrating certain festivals and believing that this will accumulate enough merit to go to the Deva realms. It is devotion, respect and gratitude to the Triple Gem which counts. This kind of belief is not confined to religious activities; everybody lives with rites and rituals, even though we may not be aware of them. In human relationships there are prescribed ways of acting in respect to our parents, children and partner. How we relate in our job to friends and strangers, how we want to be confirmed by others—all this is connected to preconceived ideas of what is right and proper in a certain culture and tradition. Yet none of it has any basic truth in it; it is all mind-made. The more ideas we have, the less we can see reality. The more we believe in them, the harder it is to abandon them. As we imagine ourselves to be a certain kind of person, one relates in that way in all situations. It isn't only how we put flowers on a shrine, it can also be how we greet people, if we do it according to a certain stereotyped ritual, and not with an open heart and mind.

These three obstructions fall away when a path- and fruit-moment has been experienced. There can be a marked change in such a person, which is not externally visible. It would be nice to wear a halo and look blissful. But the inner change is, firstly, that the experience leaves absolutely no doubt what has to be done in this life. The event is totally different from anything previously known, so much so in fact that it makes our former life, up to that point, immaterial. Nothing can be found in the past which has fundamental importance. The only significance lies in going ahead with the practice so that this minimal experience of the first path-moment can be fortified, resurrected and firmly established in ourselves.

The path- and fruit-moments recur for the Once-returner (*sakadāgāmi*), the Non-returner (*anāgāmī*) and the Enlightened One (*Arahant*), and each time they are not only deepened, but can be lengthened. We could compare this to having examinations at the university. If we are going through four years of university study to get a certain degree, we have to pass examinations at the end of each year. We have to answer questions each time, based on our previously absorbed knowledge, and the questions become deeper, more profound and more difficult with each subsequent examination. While the questions are always concerned with the same subject, they require more depth and profundity of understanding each time, until we finally graduate and don't have to return to university. It's the same with our spiritual development. Each path-moment is based on the previous one and is concerned with the same subject, yet it goes deeper and further until we pass our final test and need not return again.

The path-moment doesn't have any thinking or feeling in it. It is not comparable to the meditative absorptions (*jhāna*), although it is based upon them and only the concentrated mind can enter into a path-moment. It differs in that it does not have the same qualities the meditative absorptions have, namely: in their initial stages, the ingredients of rapture, happiness and peacefulness; and later on, the mind experiences expansion, nothingness and a change of perception. The path-moment does not contain any of these states of mind. It has a quality of non-being. This is such a relief and changes our world view so totally that it is quite understandable that the Buddha made such a distinction between a worldling and a noble one. While the meditative absorptions bring with them a feeling of oneness, of unity, the path-moment does not even contain that. The moment of fruition, subsequent to the path-moment, is the understood experience, and results in a turned-around vision of existence.

The new understanding recognizes every thought and feeling as suffering (*dukkha*), even the most elevated thought or sublime feeling still has this quality. Only when there is nothing does suffering cease, nothing internal or external that contains the quality of total satisfactoriness. Because of such an inner vision, the passion for wanting anything is discarded. All has been seen for what it really is and nothing can give the happiness that arises through the practice of the path and its results.

The Nibbānic element cannot be truly described as bliss, because bliss has a connotation of exhilaration. We use the word 'bliss' for the meditative absorption, where it includes a sense of excitement, but the Nibbānic element does not recognize bliss because all that arises is seen as suffering. "The bliss of Nibbāna" may give us the impression that we may find perfect happiness, but the opposite is true. We find that there is nothing and therefore no more unhappiness, only peace. And to look for path and fruit will not bring it about, because only moment to moment awareness can do so. This awareness will eventually culminate in real concentration where we can let go of thinking and be totally absorbed, and can drop the meditation subject we have been using. We need not push it aside; it simply falls away of its own accord and absorption in awareness occurs. If we have to have an ambition in life, this is the only worthwhile one to have; all others will not bring about any fulfilment.

We don't have to force ourselves to give up sceptical doubt. What is there to doubt when we have experienced the truth? If we hit ourselves with a hammer, we feel pain and cannot doubt it. We know it from our own experience.

Rites and rituals are brought to an end because the person who has experienced a path-moment will not indulge in role-playing because all roles have the elements of unreality. We may continue with the religious rites, because they contain aspects of respect, gratitude and devotion, but there will not be any rituals in relating to people or to situations, and no inventing stories about ourselves, because our response is with a spontaneous open heart.

Letting go the wrong view of self is the most profound change, causing all other changes. For the Stream-enterer the wrong view of self can never arise again intellectually, but it can still arise feeling-wise. Because the path-moment has been so fleeting, it hasn't had the complete impact yet. Had it done so, it would have resulted in full Enlightenment. This is possible and is mentioned in the Buddha's discourses as having happened several times. Some disciples realized all four stages of holiness while listening to the Dhamma.

The initial fruit-moment needs to be relived and resurrected again and again, until the second path-moment arises. It's like repeating what we know and not forgetting the moment, so that we can build on it.

It is very useful to remind ourselves in all our waking moments that body, feeling, perception, mental formations and consciousness are all impermanent and have no core substance, changing from moment to moment. Whether we have had a direct vision of non-self (*anattā*) or just an understanding of it, either way we have to bring it back into our mind and relive it as often as possible. As we continue to do this, ordinary problems arise less and less. If we remain aware of the impermanence of all that exists, our difficulties seem far less important and the view of self subtly changes.

The view we have of ourselves is our worst enemy. Everyone has made up a persona, a mask that we wear. We don't want to see what's behind it, and we don't allow anyone else to look either. After having had a path-moment, it is no longer possible to sustain this disguise. However the mask, the fear and rejection come to the fore. The best antidote is to remember, again and again, that there's really nobody there, only phenomena, nothing more. Even though the inner vision may not be concrete enough to substantiate such a claim, the affirmation helps to loosen the grasping and clinging, and to hang on a little less tightly.

Path and Fruit

The direction of the practice is certainly towards Stream-entry, but there's nothing to 'get,' only things to give up. Unless that is done, the moment cannot happen, and we will continue to live in the same way we always have: beset and obstructed by *dukkha*, subject to praise and blame, loss and gain, fame and ill-fame, happiness and unhappiness. The usual problems—all caused by the 'self'—will arise again and again. Real change comes when there is a decisive alteration in the way we view ourselves; otherwise the difficulties remain the same because the same identical person is generating them.

Being mindfully aware in and out of meditation is the practice which will bring results, which means doing one thing at a time, attentive to mind and body. When listening to Dhamma, for example, only listen; when sitting in meditation, only attend to the meditation subject; when planting a tree, only plant. No frills, no judgments. That habituates the mind to be in each moment. Only in such a way can a path-moment occur. It's not in the distant future; it's possible here and now. There's no reason why an intelligent, healthy, committed person should not be able to attain it with patience and perseverance.

We have heard about disenchantment and dispassion as steps on the path to liberation and freedom. They cannot have meaning and impact unless there is a vision of a totally different reality, one which does not contain the world's manifoldness. When we sit in meditation and start thinking about worldly things, that's the temptation of diversification and expansion (*papañca*). The Nibbāna element is one, not manifold. We could say that it is empty of all that we know. Until that is seen, the

All of Us

world will keep calling, but we need not believe it all. It is a difficult task, so we have to remind ourselves often, otherwise we get caught up by temptation. We should not be surprised when we don't find happiness. Manifoldness, diversification cannot create happiness, only distraction.

Certainly, we can experience pleasure from the senses. If we have good *kamma*, there will be many such occasions: good food, beautiful scenery, pleasant people, good music, interesting books, a comfortable home, not too much physical discomfort. But do these bring fulfilment? Since it didn't happen in the past, why should it occur in the future? Path and fruit bring fulfilment because they are empty of phenomena. Emptiness does not change nor does it become unpleasant and it cannot lack peace, since there is nothing to disturb it.

When people hear or read about Nibbāna, they are apt to say: "How can I want nothing?" When we have seen that everything we can possibly want is meant to fill an inner void of dissatisfaction, then the time has come to want nothing. This goes beyond 'not wanting' because we now accept the reality that there is nothing worthwhile to be had. Not wanting anything will make it possible to experience that there is actually nothing—only peace and quiet.

GLOSSARY

The following Pali words encompass concepts and levels of ideas for which there are no adequate synonyms in English. The explanations of these terms have been adapted from the *Buddhist Dictionary* by Nyanatiloka Mahāthera.

Anāgāmi: The Non-Returner is a noble disciple on the third stage of enlightenment

Anattā: Not-self, non-ego, egolessness, impersonality. Neither within nor outside the bodily and mental phenomena of existence can be found anything that in the ultimate sense could be regarded as a permanent, self-existing, real ego-identity, soul, or any other abiding substance.

Anicca: Impermanence; a basic feature of all conditioned phenomena, be they material or mental, coarse or subtle, internal or external.

Anusaya: The seven proclivities, inclinations or tendencies.

Arahat/Arahant: The Enlightened One. Through the extinction of all cankers, he reaches already in this very life the deliverance of mind, the deliverance through wisdom, which is free from cankers, and which he himself has understood and realized.

Ariya: Noble ones or noble persons.

Avijjā: Ignorance, nescience, unknowing. Synonymous with delusion, it is the primary root of all evil and suffering in the world, veiling one's mental eyes and preventing one from seeing the impermanent, suffering, and not-self nature of things.

Bhavarāga: Craving for existence; one of the seven tendencies.

Cittaviveka: Mental detachment; the inner detachment from sensuous things.

Deva: Heavenly being, deity, god; a celestial being who lives in a happy world, but is not freed from the cycle of existence.

Dhamma: (1) Capital *Dhamma* means the liberating law discovered and proclaimed by the Buddha, summed up in the Four Noble Truths.

ù(2) Lower case *dhamma* is a mental phenomenon, in relation to the mind sphere as part of the six sense-spheres.

Diṭṭhi: View, belief, speculative opinion. If not qualified by 'right,' it mostly refers to wrong and evil view or opinion.

Dukkha: (1) In common usage: pain, painful feeling, which may be bodily or mental.

—(2) In Buddhist usage as, e.g. in the Four Noble Truths: suffering, ill, the unsatisfactory nature, and general insecurity of all conditioned phenomena.

Jhāna: Meditative absorptions. Tranquillity meditation.

Kalyāṇamitta: A noble or good friend who is a senior monk, who is also the mentor and friend of his pupil, who cares about his welfare and progress, and in particular acts as his meditation teacher.

Kamma/Karma: Action. It denotes the wholesome and unwholesome volitions and their concomitant mental factors, causing rebirth and shaping the character of beings and thereby their destiny. The term does not

Glossary

signify the result of actions and most certainly not the deterministic fate of man.

Kammaṭṭhāna: Lit. 'working-ground' (i.e. for meditation). It is the term for subjects of meditation used in the commentaries.

Kāya-viveka: Bodily detachment, i.e. abiding in solitude free from alluring sensuous objects.

Khandha: The five 'groups.' They are five aspects in which the Buddha has summed up all the physical and mental phenomena of existence, and which appear to the ordinary person as his self or personality, namely: body, feeling, perception, mental formations, and consciousness.

Lokiya: 'mundane,' are all those states of consciousness and mental factors arising in the worldling, as well as in the noble one, which are not associated with the supramundane (*lokuttara*).

Lokuttara: 'supramundane,' is a term for the four paths and four fruitions.

Magga-phala: Path and fruit. The path of consciousness arises first; according to the commentaries it is immediately followed by 'fruition,' a moment of supramundane awareness.

Māna: Conceit or pride. One of the ten fetters binding one to existence; also one of the underlying tendencies.

Māra: The Buddhist 'tempter' figure, the personification of evil and the passions, of the totality of worldly existence and of death.

Mettā: Loving-kindness is one of the four sublime emotions (*brahma-vihāra*).

Nibbāna: Lit. 'extinction,' to cease blowing, to become extinguished. Nibbāna constitutes the highest and ultimate goal of all Buddhist aspirations, i.e., absolute extinction of that life-affirming will, manifest as greed, hate and delusion, and clinging to existence; thereby the absolute deliverance from all future rebirth.

Nīvaraṇa: 'Hindrances;' the five qualities which are obstacles to the mind and blind our mental vision, obstructing concentration, namely: sensual desire, ill will, sloth and torpor, restlessness and worry, and sceptical doubt.

Papañca: Proliferation, expansion, diffuseness, manifoldness, elaboration, differentiation. Denotes the mental tendency to elaborate on things because of craving, conceit, and views. More specifically, the tendency to create a 'self' out of a sense-experience.

Paṭiccasamuppāda: 'Dependent Origination;' the doctrine of the conditionality of all physical and mental phenomena. It starts with ignorance and ends with suffering.

Puthujjana: Lit. 'one of the many folk,' worldling, ordinary man. Anyone still possessed of the ten fetters binding to the round of rebirths.

Sacca: Truth, such as the 'Four Noble Truths.'.

Sakadāgāmi: Once-Returner. A noble person who has abandoned the lower fetters and has diminished anger.

Sakkāya-diṭṭhi: Personality-belief. It is the first of the ten fetters and is abandoned at Stream-entry.

Samatha: Tranquillity, or serenity. A synonym of *samādhi* (concentration).

Saṃsāra: Round of rebirth, lit. 'perpetual wandering,' a name for the "sea of life ever restlessly heaving up and down," and, in a more specific sense, wandering

Glossary

from birth to birth in various realms of existence.

Sangha: Lit. 'congregation;' the name for the community of monks and nuns. As the third of the Three Gems and the Three Refuges, it applies to the community of the noble ones.

Saṃvega: 'the sources of emotion,' or a sense of urgency.

Saṅkhāra: Most general usage is formations: mental formations and kamma formations. Sometimes also meaning bodily or mental functions; or anything formed.

Sīlabbata-parāmāsa: Attachment to mere rules and rituals; the third fetter and one of the four kinds of clinging. It disappears on attaining to Stream-entry. [Lit. "attachment to virtues (*sīla*) and vows (*vata*)." "Rules and rituals" is a common but incorrect translation arising out of misunderstanding by Victorian translators. BPS ed.]

Sotāpatti: Stream-entry, the first attainment of becoming a noble one.

Sotāpanna: Stream-Enterer, one who has attained Stream-entry.

Vicikicchā: Sceptical doubt; one of the five mental hindrances and one of the three fetters, which disappears forever at Stream-entry.

Vipassanā: Insight into the truth of the impermanence, suffering and impersonality of all corporeal and mental phenomena of existence.

Yathā-bhūta-ñāṇa-dassana: The knowledge and vision according to reality, seeing things as they are, seeing things in accordance with the Four Noble Truths and the characteristics of impermanence, suffering, and not-self.

Of Related Interest

MEDITATION
Talks on Meditation
Ajahn Chah

This compilation consists of five talks and three question and answer sessions by the renowned Thai Forest Tradition teacher Venerable Ajahn Chah. The selected talks mainly deal with the topic of meditation, both tranquillity meditation as well as insight meditation. Ajahn Chah discusses the beginning steps as well as the higher stages and this book is a source of inspiration for beginners as well as serious practitioners.

BP 519S 158pp.

WITHIN OUR OWN HEARTS
Ayyā Khemā

This little volume of Dhamma talks offered here to show a way out of our problems and sufferings, to give an idea of the Buddha's way to reach ultimate peace and happiness. If anyone becomes inspired to practice this path of moral conduct, meditation and insight, our world will be so much the better for it.

This inspiring book is based on twelve talks given at the Parappaduwa Nuns Island in Sri Lanka. Ayyā Khemā insists that the Buddha's teachings, though profound, are simple and can be realized within our own hearts.

BP 518S 134 pp.

Prices according to latest catalogue (http://www.bps.lk)

THE BUDDHIST PUBLICATION SOCIETY

The BPS is an approved charity dedicated to making known the Teaching of the Buddha, which has a vital message for all people.

Founded in 1958, the BPS has published a wide variety of books and booklets covering a great range of topics. Its publications include accurate annotated translations of the Buddha's discourses, standard reference works, as well as original contemporary expositions of Buddhist thought and practice. These works present Buddhism as it truly is—a dynamic force which has influenced receptive minds for the past 2500 years and is still as relevant today as it was when it first arose.

For more information about the BPS and our publications, please visit our website, or write an e-mail, or a letter to the:

Administrative Secretary
Buddhist Publication Society
P.O. Box 61
54 Sangharaja Mawatha
Kandy • Sri Lanka
E-mail: bps@bps.lk
web site: http://www.bps.lk
Tel: 0094 81 223 7283 • Fax: 0094 81 222 3679